Yuri Norstein and *Tale of Tales*

An Animator's Journey

CLARE KITSON

Cataloguing in Publication Data
A catalogue record for this book is available from the British Library

Yuri Norstein and *Tale of Tales*: An Animator's Journey

ISBN: 0 86196 646 5 (Paperback)

Frontispiece opposite: Yuri Norstein [Photo Larisa Pankratova].

Published by
John Libbey Publishing, Box 276, Eastleigh SO50 5YS, UK
e-mail: john.libbey@libertysurf.fr; web site: www.johnlibbey.com

Orders (outside US): Book Representation & Distribution Ltd:
info@bookreps.com

Co-published in North America by
Indiana University Press, 601 North Morton St, Bloomington, IN 47404, USA
www.iupress.indiana.edu

Distributed in Australasia by
Elsevier Australia, 30-52 Smidmore Street, Marrickville NSW 2204, Australia

Printed in Malaysia by Vivar Printing Sdn. Bhd., 48000 Rawang,
Selangor Darul Ehsan.

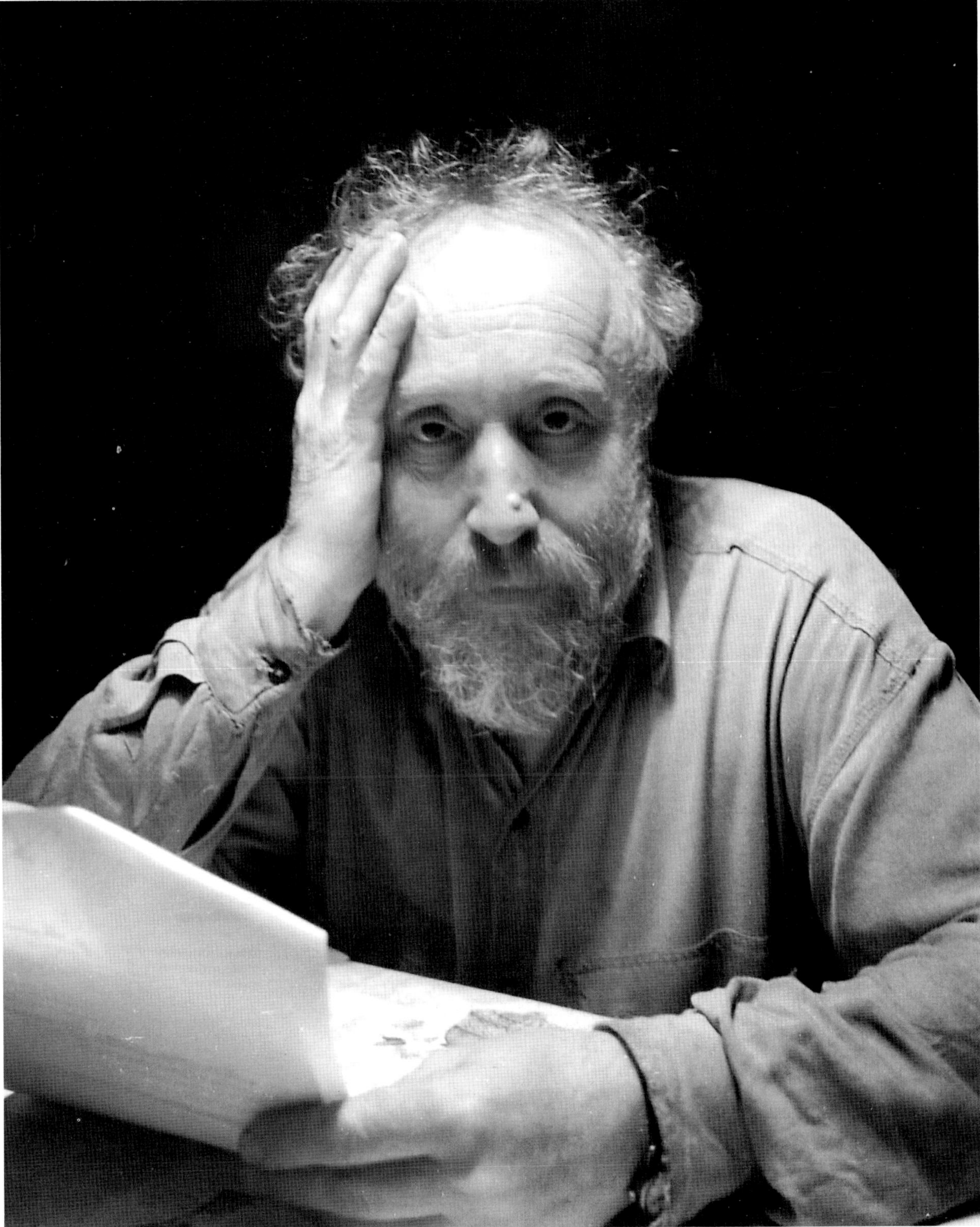

Contents

Foreword

I've loved the films of Yuri Norstein for years now. I first saw *Tale of Tales* and his earlier *Hedgehog in the Fog* as a film student in the early 1980s and became instantly enchanted. Like many I was immediately drawn into his sensual world by the richness of the aural and visual landscapes he creates. Norstein's films are magical and atmospheric, lovingly and masterfully executed using multi-layered, back and front lit cut-out animation. His story-telling and illustration style is earthy and rich in symbols which are beautiful in themselves – but one senses there is a lot more hidden behind them that a Western European mind cannot fully see.

I'm so glad Clare Kitson, through this book, has sought to shed light on an artist and animator so deserving and so little known outside his field, particularly in the West. Rather than over-explain Norstein's work, and in any way spoil the magic, she takes us on a journey through his life in the post-war Soviet Union, colouring in the background and providing a context that helps us understand the often paradoxical circumstances in and through which he flourished.

I've known Clare Kitson for many years. Her knowledge of Russia and of Norstein's life and work is impressive. But above all she is, like me, enchanted by his spell.

Nick Park CBE

Acknowledgements

Many authors use the phrase 'without whose help this book would not have been possible'. In my case this is the literal truth. Without the Surrey Institute of Art & Design, University College, I would never have had the opportunity to write this book. Many people at the Institute have helped in many ways, but I must single out the late Jill McGreal, whose brainchild the Animation Research Centre was, who offered me this research opportunity and then persuaded me that I could make the material into a book; Roger Noake; Dr Suzanne Buchan; and Professor Manuel Alvarado, who has been an unfailing source of support.

Two more 'without whom ...'s are of course John Libbey, who had the faith to publish a work that inhabits a small, if endlessly fascinating, niche, and Professor Geoffrey Nowell-Smith, who helped to pull it into shape.

My translations of Lyudmila Petrushevskaya's proposal and treatment for *Tale of Tales* owe much to the advice of Dr Linda Aldwinckle of the University of Westminster, who supervised my MA translation project based on these and other *Tale of Tales*-related texts, and input from Layla Alexander and Natasha Synessios.

Natasha has also generously given time to read and comment on my manuscript, as have Derek Hill, John Jordan, Dr Andreas Weitzer, Ruth Lingford and Professor Julian Graffy.

I have to thank Joan Borsten of Films By Jove, Jacques Souffre of A.K. Vidéo, Mikiko Takeda of Studio Ghibli, Kosei Miya and Misha Berkovsky for their precious help in accessing the illustrations which are so crucial to this book.

Finally, the many people in Moscow who facilitated my task: Naum Kleiman and Sveta Kim of the Cinema Museum, who would always manage to find in their files just the piece of artwork or the document I was looking for; Natasha Abramova, who likewise offered access to some unique correspondence as well as giving up her time to be interviewed, along with Norstein himself, Francesca Yarbusova, Lyudmila Petrushevskaya, Igor Skidan-Bosin and Alexander Kalyagin. Several friends, notably Sonya Berkovskaya, Kostya Kvitko and Zhenya Beginin, solved my practical problems.

But most of all I have to thank Yuri Norstein and his whole team, but especially Tanya Usvaiskaya, Maxim Granik and Valya Olshvang, who have always made me feel so very welcome at the studio and never resented the time spent servicing my needs. Norstein has been particularly generous, submitting to long interviews, hunting out photographs and sketches and answering a mountain of faxed queries. His patience attained especially heroic proportions during the latter stages when, attempting to put together a complete filmography, I had to ask him to adjudicate between various contradictory sources, forcing him to re-live the frustrations of his protracted early career as an animator on other directors' not very good films. After pages-long and rather terrifying tirades, he would nevertheless always reassure me: 'Anything else you need to know – don't be shy to ask!'

Language note

Partly in deference to non-Russianist readers, and partly because I am not proficient in the system used by academics, I have used here a simplified transliteration system (the main area of simplification being the elimination of hard and soft signs, and of double vowels at the ends of names and adjectives, where these do not affect the pronunciation).

Where names have English or other more familiar equivalents, I have used these (e.g. Alexander, Edward, Francesca) rather than transliterations from the Russian.

Likewise, for the names of Russians living abroad I have used whatever Roman alphabet spelling they themselves have adopted.

Clare Kitson
February 2005

1

Why a book?

What sort of animal was it, then, living in that abandoned house and roasting potatoes, burning its fingers (paws?) as it ate them? And who was that old woman, suddenly popping up in the middle of the abandoned house to stoke the fire? What was that all about? These were the kinds of not very profound questions that exercised audiences at the 1980 Zagreb International Animation Festival, as they tried to get to grips with *Tale of Tales*.

Festival-goers are a motley crew – predominantly filmmakers, but including a fair sprinkling of hangers-on (including myself) from other festivals, television and a variety of organisations that programme animation. And a few journalists, but never enough to spread the animation gospel

Fig. 1. The Little Wolf looks out from the abandoned house.
[Courtesy Films By Jove]

effectively ... As a group they have no trouble singling out the films that have any chance of a prize, and getting a feel for the event as a whole via exchanges of views with friends and colleagues. Some festivals have plenty of good films but nothing of the stature for an obvious Grand Prix winner. But at this festival one film stood out. Everyone was talking about it. The main prize just had to go to this half-hour Russian film. Despite its mysteries, everyone sensed that this poetic, wistful work, full of idiosyncratic humour, was a masterpiece.

Of course the Russians at the festival, and others who knew the country well, realised there were some far more pertinent issues. They had no trouble recognising the wolf. From the first strains of that lullaby they knew so well, 'The Little Grey Wolf Will Come', they were prepared for that creature to appear and whisk them off, to immerse them in memories of their own childhood. No, the more interesting questions were: What sort of Russian could think of making such a truly original film at this time? And, perhaps even more pertinently: How did he manage to get away with it? For we were still in the middle of the Brezhnev-era period of 'stagnation', when the dead hand of officialdom was doing its best to stifle any creativity in the USSR. Forty years on, the cultural authorities were still clinging to Stalin's precepts for Socialist Realism in the arts: optimistic tone, positive hero and a simplicity of narrative that would be understood by all. All works

Fig. 2. The results of the Olympiad of Animation poll.

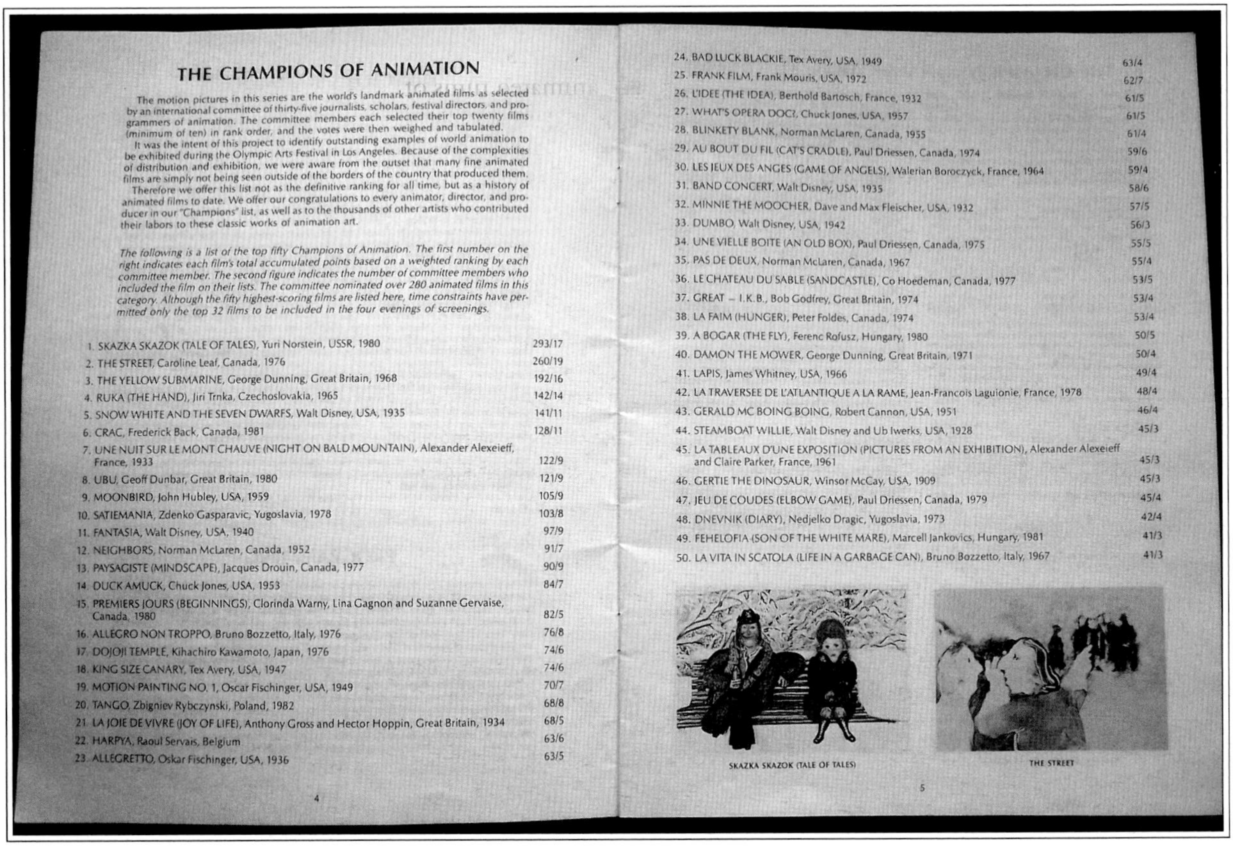

THE CHAMPIONS OF ANIMATION

The motion pictures in this series are the world's landmark animated films as selected by an international committee of thirty-five journalists, scholars, festival directors, and programmers of animation. The committee members each selected their top twenty films (minimum of ten) in rank order, and the votes were then weighed and tabulated.

It was the intent of this project to identify outstanding examples of world animation to be exhibited during the Olympic Arts Festival in Los Angeles. Because of the complexities of distribution and exhibition, we were aware from the outset that many fine animated films are simply not being seen outside of the borders of the country that produced them.

Therefore we offer this list not as the definitive ranking for all time, but as a history of animated films to date. We offer our congratulations to every animator, director, and producer in our "Champions" list, as well as to the thousands of other artists who contributed their labors to these classic works of animation art.

The following is a list of the top fifty Champions of Animation. The first number on the right indicates each film's total accumulated points based on a weighted ranking by each committee member. The second figure indicates the number of committee members who included the film on their lists. The committee nominated over 280 animated films in this category. Although the fifty highest-scoring films are listed here, time constraints have permitted only the top 32 films to be included in the four evenings of screenings.

1. SKAZKA SKAZOK (TALE OF TALES), Yuri Norstein, USSR, 1980	293/17
2. THE STREET, Caroline Leaf, Canada, 1976	260/19
3. THE YELLOW SUBMARINE, George Dunning, Great Britain, 1968	192/16
4. RUKA (THE HAND), Jiri Trnka, Czechoslovakia, 1965	142/14
5. SNOW WHITE AND THE SEVEN DWARFS, Walt Disney, USA, 1935	141/11
6. CRAC, Frederick Back, Canada, 1981	128/11
7. UNE NUIT SUR LE MONT CHAUVE (NIGHT ON BALD MOUNTAIN), Alexander Alexeieff, France, 1933	122/9
8. UBU, Geoff Dunbar, Great Britain, 1980	121/9
9. MOONBIRD, John Hubley, USA, 1959	105/9
10. SATIEMANIA, Zdenko Gasparavic, Yugoslavia, 1978	103/8
11. FANTASIA, Walt Disney, USA, 1940	97/9
12. NEIGHBORS, Norman McLaren, Canada, 1952	91/7
13. PAYSAGISTE (MINDSCAPE), Jacques Drouin, Canada, 1977	90/9
14. DUCK AMUCK, Chuck Jones, USA, 1953	84/7
15. PREMIERS JOURS (BEGINNINGS), Clorinda Warny, Lina Gagnon and Suzanne Gervaise, Canada, 1980	82/5
16. ALLEGRO NON TROPPO, Bruno Bozzetto, Italy, 1976	76/8
17. DOJOJI TEMPLE, Kihachiro Kawamoto, Japan, 1976	74/6
18. KING SIZE CANARY, Tex Avery, USA, 1947	74/6
19. MOTION PAINTING NO. 1, Oscar Fischinger, USA, 1949	70/7
20. TANGO, Zbigniev Rybczynski, Poland, 1982	68/8
21. LA JOIE DE VIVRE (JOY OF LIFE), Anthony Gross and Hector Hoppin, Great Britain, 1934	68/5
22. HARPYA, Raoul Servais, Belgium	63/6
23. ALLEGRETTO, Oskar Fischinger, USA, 1936	63/5
24. BAD LUCK BLACKIE, Tex Avery, USA, 1949	63/4
25. FRANK FILM, Frank Mouris, USA, 1972	62/7
26. L'IDEE (THE IDEA), Berthold Bartosch, France, 1932	61/5
27. WHAT'S OPERA DOC?, Chuck Jones, USA, 1957	61/5
28. BLINKETY BLANK, Norman McLaren, Canada, 1955	61/4
29. AU BOUT DU FIL (CAT'S CRADLE), Paul Driessen, Canada, 1974	59/6
30. LES JEUX DES ANGES (GAME OF ANGELS), Walerian Boroczyck, France, 1964	59/4
31. BAND CONCERT, Walt Disney, USA, 1935	58/6
32. MINNIE THE MOOCHER, Dave and Max Fleischer, USA, 1932	57/5
33. DUMBO, Walt Disney, USA, 1942	56/3
34. UNE VIELLE BOITE (AN OLD BOX), Paul Driessen, Canada, 1975	55/5
35. PAS DE DEUX, Norman McLaren, Canada, 1967	55/4
36. LE CHATEAU DU SABLE (SANDCASTLE), Co Hoedeman, Canada, 1977	53/5
37. GREAT – I.K.B., Bob Godfrey, Great Britain, 1974	53/4
38. LA FAIM (HUNGER), Peter Foldes, Canada, 1974	53/4
39. A BOGAR (THE FLY), Ferenc Rofusz, Hungary, 1980	50/5
40. DAMON THE MOWER, George Dunning, Great Britain, 1971	50/4
41. LAPIS, James Whitney, USA, 1966	49/4
42. LA TRAVERSEE DE L'ATLANTIQUE A LA RAME, Jean-Francois Laguionie, France, 1978	48/4
43. GERALD MC BOING BOING, Robert Cannon, USA, 1951	46/4
44. STEAMBOAT WILLIE, Walt Disney and Ub Iwerks, USA, 1928	45/3
45. LA TABLEAUX D'UNE EXPOSITION (PICTURES FROM AN EXHIBITION), Alexander Alexeieff and Claire Parker, France, 1961	45/3
46. GERTIE THE DINOSAUR, Winsor McCay, USA, 1909	45/3
47. JEU DE COUDES (ELBOW GAME), Paul Driessen, Canada, 1979	45/4
48. DNEVNIK (DIARY), Nedjelko Dragic, Yugoslavia, 1973	42/4
49. FEHELOFIA (SON OF THE WHITE MARE), Marcell Jankovics, Hungary, 1981	41/3
50. LA VITA IN SCATOLA (LIFE IN A GARBAGE CAN), Bruno Bozzetto, Italy, 1967	41/3

SKAZKA SKAZOK (TALE OF TALES)

THE STREET

4

5

of art were supposed to be scrutinised during the course of production for any sign of originality, which would immediately be excised. Yet *Tale of Tales* did not fit the mould in any respect. Its tone was melancholy, its structure complex and the overall effect quite unique. Hence the *frisson* of expectation at the awards ceremony – not so much anticipation of discovering the winning film, but curiosity as to what sort of Russian might have had the originality, not to mention the temerity ...

Sure enough, after the other prizes had been announced, we learned that 'The winner of the Grand Prix is ... Yuri Norstein, for *Tale of Tales*'. But, of course, no Yuri Norstein appeared. Instead it was one of the many bureaucrats-*cum*-KGB men that peopled the Soviet film distribution scene at that period. We should have remembered: this same Yuri Norstein's previous short films, *The Fox and the Hare*, *The Heron and the Crane* and *Hedgehog in the Fog* had also garnered a good few festival prizes – but Norstein had never been on hand to pick them up. This was not because he was too busy, or because he could not afford the fare. In the Soviet Union the State Committee for Cinematography (Goskino) decided who should travel and who should not. Many filmmakers did: Yuri Norstein emphatically did not.

Tale of Tales pursued its triumphant course, taking more awards, at Oberhausen, Ottawa, Lille and others. Most films, even mega-awardwinners, have a natural life span and are largely forgotten once they have completed the festival circuit. Not so *Tale of Tales*. Four years later, when the Olympics were held in Los Angeles, the local animation aficionados decided to organise a parallel Olympiad of Animation. The event featured an extremely scientific survey to establish the champion animated films of all time. An international panel of 35 judges – critics, academics, festival directors and other knowledgeable types – were asked to list, in rank order, their top twenty animated films. When the results were weighted and tabulated, *Tale of Tales* came top.[1]

A far more modest UK survey, taken by the Channel 4 animation magazine show *Dope Sheet* in 1997, came to the same conclusion. And, to clinch it, that same Zagreb Festival, scene of *Tale of Tales*' first glorious outing, recently organised a far broader, and perhaps more democratic poll than the LA study. Over a period of four years mini-polls were conducted both during the festival and within local groups of the International Animated Film Association (comprising animators, other related professionals but also fans). When the short list was announced, it was considerably different from that of the Olympiad. Apart from anything else, a new generation of filmmakers was now in the running, including Nick Park, creator of Wallace and Gromit and *Chicken Run*, and those titans of experimental cinema the brothers Quay. Yet the result, announced in June 2002, showed that *Tale of Tales* was still top.

Unlike Disney features and Japanese *anime*, *Tale of Tales* has had no massive marketing department behind it. Nor has it had any state support on its international outings from Goskino's cultural relations department. Even within the Soviet Union, journalists from large-circulation periodicals were 'discouraged' from writing about the film. It has therefore been seen by relatively few people. Yet it manages to inspire all who do see

1 To provide some context: Caroline Leaf's *The Street* was second and George Dunning's *Yellow Submarine* third. Jiří Trnka made number four with *The Hand*, Disney five with *Snow White* and Chuck Jones number 14 with *Duck Amuck*. Seventeen of the 35 respondents cited *Tale of Tales* (only one film was cited by a higher number) and its average weighted score was a staggering 17.2 out of 20.

Fig. 3. Norstein in 2004 with colleagues Tanya Usvaiskaya and Larisa Zenevich, and Pirat. [Photo Clare Kitson]

it – even those who, like me, have struggled a bit with the presumed metaphors behind it. I might, incidentally, have panicked less about my inability to penetrate all the film's secrets, had I known then what I only recently discovered: Lyudmila Petrushevskaya, who wrote the script based on Norstein's ideas, was equally puzzled. In a letter addressed to Norstein, in the catalogue for a French exhibition of his and his designer wife's work, she tells him: 'Only when you had finished shooting the film did I begin to grasp your idea. I have seen *Tale of Tales* no less than fifty times. But the mystery never goes away.'[2]

It was certainly the puzzlement factor which, initially, accounted for my own fascination with the film. Shortly after first seeing it I was in Moscow researching a Soviet animation season for the National Film Theatre when I first managed to make contact with the elusive Norstein. (Not, of course, through official channels but via the standard Soviet network of friends of friends …) I was nervous at the prospect of meeting the creative genius behind such a film, especially since he had obviously managed to make himself so very unpopular with the authorities. In the event, I was somewhat disconcerted to meet what appeared to be one of the most ordinary, relaxed, cheerful, sociable, joke-telling dinner companions I had come across in Moscow. Neither a tortured artist nor a bitter and twisted victim. Sadly, the jokes went over my head, being beyond the capacity of the friends who were acting as interpreters. This dinner was a contributory factor to my buying, that same year, the wonderful *Teach Yourself Russian* and embarking on two decades of determined study.

2 *Yuri Norstein, Francesca Yarbusova*, Hôtel de Ville de Paris, Paris 2001, p. 189.

Fig. 4. Fedor Khitruk with his wife Galina in 2000. [Photo Clare Kitson]

But while my language studies advanced fairly rapidly, and while from then on I regularly saw Norstein on my trips to Moscow (but not in London – he was not allowed to come in 1983 for that NFT season), my *Tale of Tales* project had to be put on hold. I had a living to earn. Not until 1999, when I was offered a part-time research post at the Surrey Institute of Art & Design, University College, and the opportunity to research whatever animation topic took my fancy, did I get my chance to find out more about the filmmaker and the film. In April 2000, together with my Surrey Institute colleague Roger Noake, I went to Moscow to interview Norstein in depth, as well as all other surviving members of the production team.

Two things became clear. One was that the story of the film's gestation, production, delivery to the authorities, banning and subsequent grudging acceptance, accompanied by much skulduggery (on both sides), was almost as dramatic as the film itself. For this work, which so intrigued international audiences, was also profoundly mysterious to the censors. And the censors were, unlike audiences, allergic to mystery. If they could not understand it, they reasoned, it just might be seditious.[3] The other thing we learned was that the film and the man were synonymous. That despite significant input from his excellent team, including notably his co-writer, the then-banned but now celebrated novelist and playwright Lyudmila Petrushevskaya, and his designer Francesca Yarbusova, this work turns out to be completely autobiographical. It is a film about memory and it contains evocative motifs from Norstein's post-war Moscow childhood. But there is far more of his life in there than just these motifs, and on many different levels.

During my 2000 Moscow visit, there was an exhibition at the Cinema Museum devoted to the 20th anniversary of *Tale of Tales*. I walked round

3 One is reminded of the British Board of Film Censors' celebrated reaction to Germaine Dulac's 1928 experimental film *The Seashell and the Clergyman*: 'It is so cryptic as to be meaningless. If there is a meaning it is doubtless objectionable.'

it with Fedor Khitruk, the doyen of Russian animation, the lone voice of innovation in the early 1960s and a great supporter of Norstein in the *débâcle* following the film's delivery to the authorities. At that time he had been the prime mover in what Petrushevskaya picturesquely calls the 'mafia of decent folk'[4], who managed to outwit the authorities by exercising an equal if not greater degree of manipulation and obfuscation. Khitruk likens *Tale of Tales* to an iceberg. About 10 per cent of its content is visible. The rest is unseen, but without it there would be no iceberg, and no film.

I have not attempted a scientific analysis of this iceberg – to do so could destroy its power. Nor have I pursued a thorough interpretation of any apparent metaphors. Norstein himself dismisses the idea of metaphor in his work which is, he claims, what the software salesmen used to call WYSYWYG – What You See Is What You Get: 'First I made the film, then I found out it was a metaphor! But for me it's all reality'.[5] And in a very real sense it is.

What I have tried to demonstrate is, firstly, how the visible 10 per cent of the iceberg made its way into the film – how some of the visual and aural motifs which perhaps to a Western audience are among the most puzzling elements are in fact the kind of everyday reality that is easily recognisable to Russians, especially those of Norstein's generation. I have also looked at the invisible 90 per cent of the iceberg: those outside influences, political, social and cultural, that affected Norstein's creative and strategic choices and thence fed into the film. I look at his turbulent experiences with the studio bosses and with Goskino on his earlier films and during the production of *Tale of Tales*, and at his (in some cases equally turbulent) relationships with his collaborators, all of which likewise left a profound mark on the film. I also try to shed light on the aesthetic and technical processes that give the film its unique appearance.

The starting point for my voyage of discovery into *Tale of Tales* was a document, headed 'Epigraph', which I found in Norstein's files, and for which we have to thank the ever-suspicious State Committee for Cinematography. There were, it seems, a good many meetings after the film was completed, during which Goskino tried to persuade Norstein and his script editor to make the film more transparent. One such meeting produced from Norstein a preamble to prepare viewers for what they were to expect in the film. Needless to say, the epigraph never made it into the film – for Norstein very specifically did not want too much transparency – but it proved a great boon to me in my research:

> At the end of the war my aunt came home from the front. She had just lost her baby, and she suggested I should be given the milk she was still producing. I was four years old then.
>
> Before I went to sleep, my mother used to sing the lullaby 'The Little Grey Wolf Will Come'. At the end of the corridor was a door leading to the street. And it seemed to me that there, waiting beyond the door, was eternal happiness, light, a talking cat and bread sprinkled with sugar.

4 She uses the phrase in a German documentary about Fedor Khitruk, *Der Hauch des kleinen Gottes*, dir. Otto Alder, prod. Tag/Traum Film- und Fernsehproduktion 1999.

5 Interview with Yuri Norstein, 15 April 2000, Moscow.

> I did not know then that in reality only our memories can be eternal. That is where everything ends up that you remember all your life. The soldiers who failed to make it back from the war. The tree under your window. The Little Wolf mother used to sing about. And the light at the end of the corridor.

We see, in the film, this dark corridor of Norstein's childhood home, and the light at the end of it, the glow from an idyllic world of happiness, friendship, poetry and eternal memories. We see the Little Wolf make that journey along the dark corridor into the light and we now know that Norstein also made the journey. He has travelled from a (physically dark) communal flat in a working-class suburb of Moscow via a junior art-school and animation school to become an artist. Despite – or perhaps because of – the Soviet system and considerable opposition, he has made a series of animated films which are uniquely poetic, culminating in *Tale of Tales*, widely recognised as his masterpiece.

This book accompanies him on the journey.

2

Our childhood coincided with the end of the war …

Maryina Roshcha 1943-1956

Where did all that happiness come from in those days?

Norstein was born into a working-class Moscow family – the second son – in September 1941. Germany had invaded the Soviet Union three months earlier, and the family had been evacuated to a village in Penza province (far to the east of Moscow, towards the Volga towns of Samara and Saratov). His first memories, however, are of his return to a wintry Moscow at the age of two. The family moved into a *kommunalka* (or communal flat) in an old building in Maryina Roshcha, in Moscow's northern suburbs. The house was the scene of Norstein's youth, the setting of all his childhood memories and was to be one of the main inspirations for *Tale of Tales*.

Now demolished in favour of tower blocks, the houses then were two-storey, usually built of wood, and had a more human aspect than the impersonal units that were to replace them in the 1960s and 1970s. The house in which Norstein actually lived was plastered over its wooden structure, so he based his *Tale of Tales* house on the more traditional-looking wooden one opposite. (Though in fact, by the time these buildings were demolished, the plaster had long since disappeared, revealing the wood beneath.)

There is now in Russia a universal nostalgia for such housing. Coincidentally, Maryina Roshcha is also fondly remembered in Shostakovich's musical *Moskva Cheremushki*. Commissioned as a paean to the brand-new Cheremushki high-rise estate, it actually has the transplanted tenants – when not pointing out corrupt practices in the allocation of the flats – loudly lamenting their previous, far tattier, homes in Maryina Roshcha.

To a Western viewer the house we see in the film could look somewhat rural – perhaps conveying some sort of faded grandeur. To any Russian, the house is instantly recognisable for what it was. And grand it certainly wasn't, nor indeed rural. It was typical of pre-war, urban, multi-occupancy housing.[6]

6 But built before the Revolution to house lower middle-class craftsmen, traders etc.

Fig. 5 (left). Maryina Roshcha. Front view of Norstein's old home in its prime. [Photo Norstein]

Fig. 6 (right). Maryina Roshcha. Side view of Norstein's old home, the stucco now gone. [Photo Igor Skidan-Bosin]

In April 2000, sitting with Roger Noake and myself at the kitchen table in the studio where Norstein now lives, works and loves to entertain, he answered our questions on his professional and personal life and the political and social background to the production of *Tale of Tales*. He spoke for hours on end, in detail and highly articulately, and we covered a lot of ground. But it all started with the reality of life in that *kommunalka*.

> In comparison with other communal flats we were better off than others. We had five families, that means about twenty people in the flat. But above us on the first floor there was a flat with twelve or so families. But they did have a separate kitchen. In our flat the corridor was the kitchen so there were cookers there – at the beginning paraffin stoves, then they brought gas in. That corridor was where everyone chucked their old belongings, but we cooked there too. There was no ventilation and the heat, noise and smells were terrible. We had to

Fig. 7. Norstein's street in Maryina Roshcha just before demolition. [Photo Alexander Zhukovsky]

Fig. 8. Norstein with older brother Garik in 1943.

economise with everything – we had no money – so we had one light for the whole corridor – dim, probably 25 watts, really dim, and everyone made sure that the last to leave the corridor turned out the light.[7]

Norstein's earliest memories, naturally, do not centre on the detail of the house. Yet the geography of the place and the dim internal lighting – lending an other-worldly luminosity to an open external door – were key to the childhood fantasies he would indulge in before drifting off to sleep: 'At the end of the corridor was a door leading to the street. And it seemed to me that there, waiting beyond the door, were eternal happiness, light, a talking cat and bread sprinkled with sugar …'

But if the brightness beyond the door was something to strive for, the dark warmth of that crowded flat provided a tremendous feeling of security to a toddler growing up in an atmosphere of euphoria following the end of the war. He had two loving parents and an older brother, as well as assorted idiosyncratic uncles and aunts whom he saw from time to time. No matter what the privations of life in a *kommunalka*, they could certainly not match the horrors ordinary citizens had faced during the war, when twenty million people had lost their lives, of whom over half were civilians. Such horrors are hardly imaginable to the corresponding generation of Britons. Jewish families must have felt a special relief at war's end, for in the occupied parts of the Soviet Union the Nazis had been rounding up and deporting Jews to concentration camps. And the occupiers had come very, very near to Moscow … Norstein remembers the war (just), and the 'killed in action' and 'missing in action' notices which left very few of his friends and neighbours untouched, and he remembers the veterans returning after the war, many with limbs missing. A war-time tragedy even accounted for Aunt Bella's comforting milk.

7 Interview with Yuri Norstein, 12 April 2000, Moscow.

Fig. 9. Aunt Bella in 1940.

> I remember that she had lots of milk and she had to pump it off, which she did at night for some reason. I remember waking up in the night. The nights were already quite light, it was summer, and in this half-light came the sound of the milk ... The light and the warmth of a mother's breast ... I remember the sound of the milk. I remember its taste ...[8]

For Aunt Bella had been in the air force, married there and had come home pregnant at war's end, only to lose the baby at the age of two weeks. Again, in the eyes of the infant Norstein, one element providing a strong link to the miseries of war but at the same time a strong physical feeling of security. The image of that large, rounded breast would never leave him and was to provide a major motif for the film.

There were aural stimuli too, which marked the child and which also ended up in the film. Norstein would have a lullaby sung to him every night before he went to sleep. In Russia, as in the UK, one single lullaby dominates the whole bedtime market. Just as in 'Rock-a-bye Baby', the inhabitant of the cradle in 'The Little Grey Wolf Will Come' is also threatened with a sticky end:

> Baby baby rock-a-bye
> On the edge you mustn't lie
> Or the little grey wolf will come
> And will nip you on the tum
> Tug you off into the wood
> Underneath the willow-root.[9]

This lullaby has the status of a folk-memory. Even today it is sung nightly all over Russia. Its deep-seated effect is evoked by critic Natalya Venzher, who began her review of the film:

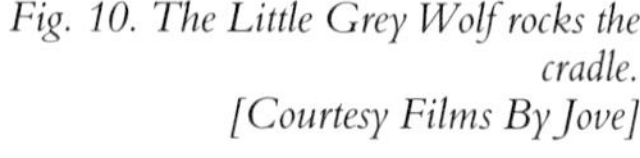

Fig. 10. The Little Grey Wolf rocks the cradle. [Courtesy Films By Jove]

8 'Dvizheniye … Glavy iz nenapisannoi knigi', Part 1, *Iskusstvo kino* 10 (1988), p. 112.

9 Translation by Gaby and Vitaly Yerenkov.

Dozing off to sleep in a warm bed, it was both sweet and scary to imagine that unknown wolf.

And later, together with many other unrealised childhood dreams the wolf was forgotten. He went off into our store of memories, to be suddenly remembered – perhaps because of a particular aroma, the scraping of a door, white muslin in a moon-beam – and he would live for a moment, bringing a sharp, physically perceptible pain in one's heart, before disappearing again for years, perhaps for ever ...[10]

Not only the song but even the wolf himself turn up in the film – providing in fact its whole structure and meaning (of which more later). But the lullaby was not the only music to influence the youthful, post-war Norstein. In fact, during the film's gestation and long before the lullaby became crucial, at a stage when the wolf was only a bit-player, Norstein had determined that the war-time tango 'Weary Sun' ('Utomlennoye solntse') [11] should play a major part, so strongly did it evoke that long-gone time. He and Petrushevskaya in fact began their 'literary' script (we would probably call it a treatment) with it:

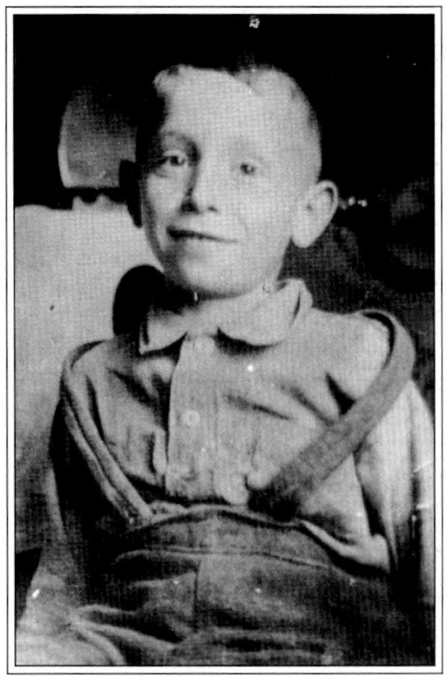

Fig. 11. Norstein photographed by his grandfather in 1946.

I don't know how it was down your way, but where we lived every evening, every summer evening – even after rain, when the sun was setting behind the clouds and a smell of wet foliage hung over the wet earth – every quiet evening when the weather was fine they used to play the tune 'Weary Sun' in the park [...]

I heard so much of that tune that it has been sounding in my ears ever since, and bringing back memories of how my Mum was young then, with shoulder-pads and funny felt boots, and how Tolya the bandit lived across the yard, 12 years old and disabled, a poor child of the war. [...]

If only we could look now, with different eyes, at the homeland of our childhood, at that cramped yard, where the earth was so trampled that the grass only pierced a way through around the edges, where the wind-blown earth floor glistened in the sun, glistened with tiny shards of glass – where did all those different-coloured bits of glass come from in those days?

And where did all that happiness come from in those days?[12]

That bedraggled yard also provided endless memories, for as the infant grew up his whole social life was indeed centred on it, with the tall poplars offering challenges to the more daring kids. Norstein spent his whole childhood in those trees. Like the lullaby, the culture of the yard is not just a Norstein memory – it is a national preoccupation. Novelist Andreï Makine, now living in France, describes an identical childhood social life with the yard as its focal point, with the same poplars and other flora. He even describes the same sounds emanating from open windows during the summer.[13] The tree that features so prominently in *Tale of Tales* is never seen full-length. To a British 'townie' this makes it hard to identify, the

10 'Zelenye yabloki na belom snegu', *Kino* (Latvia), December 1980, p. 9.

11 Written in the late 1930s by Polish composer Jerzy Petersburski as *Ta ostatnia niedziela*, Russian lyrics later added by I. Alvek. The same tune is used as the theme to Nikita Mikhalkov's Oscar-winning feature film *Utomlennye solntsem*, whose Russian title is a pun on the title of the song. This is lost in the English version, *Burnt by the Sun*.

12 See appendix for full text of treatment.

13 *Confession d'un porte-drapeau déchu*, Editions Belfond, Paris 1992, p. 10.

Fig. 12. Norstein at Maryina Roshcha, standing on the site of his home, now demolished. The poplar remains. [Photo Igor Skidan-Bosin]

only characteristic of poplars to me being their great height. I was soon put right – we are indeed dealing here with a quintessential Russian poplar.

Tolstoy believed that a person's life was divided into two parts – from birth to age five and from age five until death – and felt that the former was the more concentrated and the more important in instilling experience and forming an individual's future personality.[14] Norstein likewise feels that it was his infancy that made the biggest impression and was the major formative period for his adult life.

It was not only these conscious childhood perceptions – the music, the kids' social life centred on the yard – that would make it into the film. The colour palette of this post-war period, for example, also made an impression, if perhaps at first subliminally. Interiors were lit by 25 watt bulbs and street-lamps were also way below modern expectations. Norstein's childhood was lived in a kind of twilight, which dictated his later taste for a restricted range of colours. This is perhaps especially noticeable in *Tale of Tales*, set as it is predominantly in the immediate post-war era. (The fact that it is punctuated by a winter scene set in the present day, which is suffused – atypically for Norstein – with clear, bright colours, gives viewers a real jolt, adding to its considerable impact.)

When the teenage Norstein took up painting, it was of course the house in Maryina Roshcha that inspired his earliest efforts. One of these shows one of the neighbours in the communal flat, 'grannie Varya', against a dark background, stoking a stove, which is glowing brightly [see colour plate no. 3]. That painting later appeared in *Tale of Tales*. The way she materialises in the film [see colour plate no. 4], in the blackness of the interior, appears totally surreal to us, but in the context of the communal flat her appearance would be the most normal thing in the world. Heating was by wood-burning stoves (family members would have to bring in massive logs on carts and store them in sheds in the yard). Each family had its own stove and, in the Norsteins' building, half the families, depending on their position along the corridor, had access to their stove from their own room, whereas the others had to stoke them from outside their rooms, i.e. from the dim, windowless central corridor itself.

Incidentally, one of our conversations with Norstein revealed that grannie Varya had a son who also lived in the flat. One of Norstein's less pleasant memories, the son was a KGB employee.

These motifs from Maryina Roshcha transferred into the film as major elements in dictating an era and an atmosphere. It is worth noting that there are also various 'underwater' mini-motifs from that period of his life, largely unnoticed by audiences but of great importance to Norstein himself. An example of such a detail is the little cupboards that are revealed as part of a row of tables when, at one stage in the film, a voluminous white tablecloth is blown away. They look like bedside tables and the Russian word Norstein uses for them is indeed the word used for bedside tables (*tumbochka*). I had however been confused by some of his references to these items of furniture, and began to fear I had mis-translated the word. He said, for example, when talking about an early idea for the film, that: 'People would carry out tables, and drag out from the corridors their *tumbochki*, grey, blue, with

14 *Moya zhizn*, 1878.

Fig. 13. View along the upper corridor of Norstein's kommunalka. *(He had lived downstairs.) Note, at left below the suspended boots, two hatches allowing access to stoves. [Photo Igor Skidan-Bosin]*

oil-cloth congealed on to them, marked by knives and hot frying pans, burned by irons ...'[15] What, I wondered, were bedside tables doing in corridors, marked by knives, frying pans and irons? The answer, when it was faxed to me, was a full page long and included a labelled diagram indicating where the dishcloths hung, where the shoe-cleaning equipment was stored, etc, etc. It appears that in the cramped conditions of the

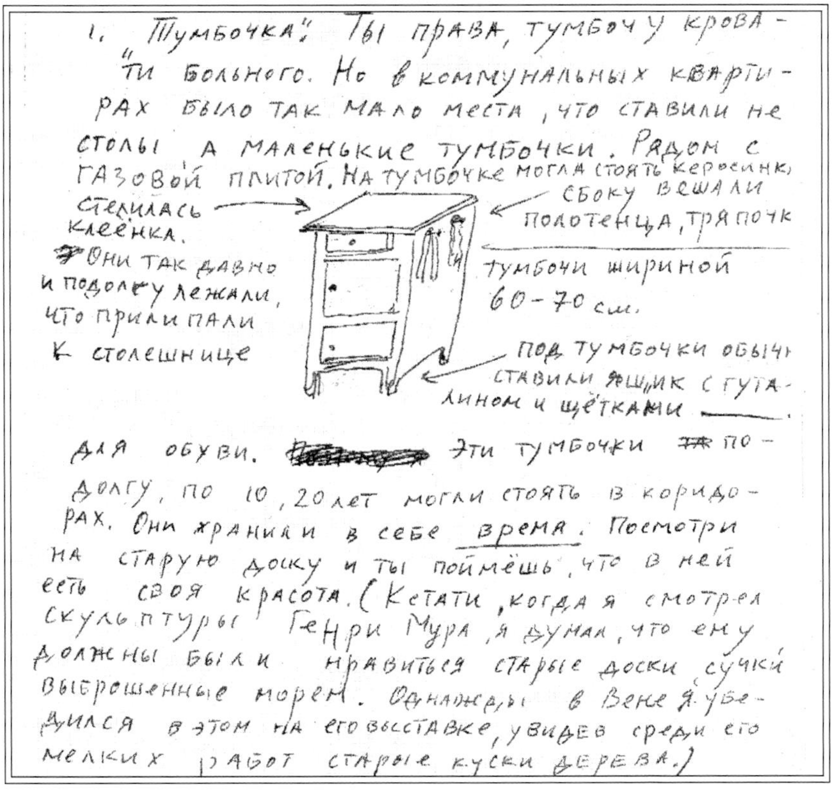

1. „Тумбочка". Ты права, тумбочку крова-
ти больного. Но в коммунальных кварти-
рах было так мало места, что ставили не
столы а маленькие тумбочки. Рядом с
газовой плитой. На тумбочке могла стоять керосинк(а)

Стелилась клеёнка.
Они так давно и подолгу лежали, что прилипали к столешнице

Сбоку вешали полотенца, тряпочк(и)

тумбочи шириной 60–70 см.

Под тумбочки обычно ставили ящик с гуталином и щётками

для обуви. Эти тумбочки по-
долгу, по 10, 20 лет могли стоять в коридо-
рах. Они хранили в себе время. Посмотри
на старую доску и ты поймёшь, что в ней
есть своя красота. (Кстати, когда я смотрел
скульптуры Генри Мура, я думал, что ему
должны были нравиться старые доски, сучки
выброшенные морем. Однажды в Вене я убе-
дился в этом на его выставке, увидев среди его
мелких работ старые куски дерева.)

Fig. 14. The multiple uses of the bedside table ... Drawing by Norstein.

15 'Metafory', Part 2, *Iskusstvo kino* 8 (1994), p. 92.

communal flats kitchen tables were out of the question. Each family instead had its multi-purpose bedside table next to the cooker. My page of explanation also included a paean to the condition of their wood after twenty years in the corridor ('They held time in their very being!') and ended 'Someone should write a poem about bedside tables. They are a part of my childhood.'

All this, and more, is in the film.

You need a great talent to live in peace-time

So life was good for the young Norstein. Yet, perhaps because those war-time memories were never far from his mind, he was always conscious of the fragility of peace and the extra burden it places on both officials and individuals. Years later, after Norstein and Petrushevskaya had written the treatment for the film, it was first discussed internally, by the studio's artistic council (comprising members of the creative staff), before being sent on to Goskino. After the main part of the discussion, Norstein was invited to speak, and he chose to emphasise this very point, the fragility of peace:

> You need a great talent to live in peace-time. For in war-time everything is intense – everything is precisely defined, clear. The personal coincides completely with the public. Everyone knows what to do and how to live. But during peace-time it's easy in your everyday life gradually to lose your way. Everything gets forgotten very quickly.[16]

And so everything had got forgotten – very quickly indeed. Norstein's earliest childhood, in the immediate aftermath of the war, had been a time of great hope for the Soviet people. After the horrors of the 1930s – the constant surveillance, the capricious imprisonments, deportations and executions – during the war Stalin had had to mellow somewhat. He now put the Party second to appeals to patriotism – for he knew his people would not give their lives for political ideology. But for their homeland they would, and did. Even enforced atheism had been put on the back burner during the war years. Immediately after the war, this loosening of discipline seemed to continue for a while – for there were new, economic problems to cope with, including a famine in 1946. The population rallied to the cause and optimism still prevailed. Later that same year, however, Stalin felt confident enough to impose a new clampdown. First it was the academics and intellectuals who suffered. There was also continuing harassment of various ethnic minorities all over the country.

This being the case, it was probably inevitable that the Jews, whose position had always been precarious, with ghettos and pogroms even under the Tsars, would be the next to suffer. The years until Stalin's providential death in 1953 were hard. Prominent Jews were singled out, publicly humiliated, falsely accused and in some cases killed. Solomon Mikhoels was a case in point. A renowned actor-director-producer, he ran the prestigious Moscow Jewish Theatre and had also set up a Jewish Anti-Fascist Committee to raise funds for the Soviet war effort, from Jews living abroad. Now, though, his theatre was trashed, his Committee dissolved and Mikhoels himself murdered by the state security service.

16 Minutes of the meeting of the artistic council of Soyuzmultfilm, 28 July 1976 (unpublished).

In late 1952 a group of doctors (mainly, but not exclusively, Jewish) were arrested on trumped-up charges of having killed or attempted to kill various Politburo members (including Stalin's ideology chief, Zhdanov) and marshals of the Soviet army. They were accused of working for US and British intelligence. Life, already uncomfortable and unpredictable for Soviet Jews, was set to get much worse, and plans were well under way to transport the whole community to Siberia. Stalin died, however, on 5 March 1953, before this plan could be put into action. The 'doctors' plot' also came to nothing since the trials did not now take place – and the doctors were finally officially exonerated.[17]

The Norstein family was Jewish and indeed Norstein's father, growing up in the 1910s and 1920s, had studied at the *heder* (or religious school), knew ancient Hebrew and read the Talmud and the Torah. By the time of Yuri's childhood under strictly enforced atheism, such an upbringing would have been completely impossible. Yet the lack of any such religious background or culture seems not to have worried him at all – he has no interest in formal religion of any persuasion, except as regards the art it produces. He was also spared much of the official anti-Semitism, since his parents took considerable trouble to keep from him the worst of the excesses. It was only much later, for example, that he heard about the transports already prepared to deport all Jews to Siberia.

His only experience of institutional anti-Semitism was an event which had initially seemed to set him on his chosen creative path, only to dash his hopes a few months later. At the age of 11 or 12, he was nominated by his art teacher at school to study for three hours, twice a week, at a special institute where trainee teachers honed their skills on talented children. The precocious Norstein, in a class of 15 and 16 year-olds, had flourished.

> I'd just begun to understand what drawing really was. But suddenly one day a teacher told me not to come back any more. I asked why and she said my work was bad. But in fact I'd only ever got good marks. It was the end of 1952, the time the 'doctors' plot' was beginning. I got home and cried my eyes out. Mum didn't say anything. I worked it all out for myself later on.[18]

It was inevitable that the anti-Semitism practised at the highest levels of authority would filter down to street level, especially where a population was suffering, and perhaps looking for scapegoats and for means of improving their own prestige in a Party-dominated society.

Norstein was badly scarred by these youthful experiences, so much so that in 1993 he wrote to a newspaper that was researching the issue. In the letter he confirms that he has been the subject of anti-Semitism, 'just as any other Jew living in the Soviet Union has'. Acknowledging that he had been spared the worst of the State-sponsored atrocities, he talks about the:

> … everyday, street-level kind [of anti-Semitism]. The kind you get in your flat or your *kommunalka*, or at school from your contemporaries. It was automatic, mindless, a reflex action. […] But how can

17 More detail on Soviet postwar history: *Encyclopaedia Britannica* (1999 edn): Union of Soviet Socialist Republics: Postwar.

18 Interview with Yuri Norstein, 12 April 2000, Moscow.

Fig. 15. Norstein's preliminary drawing for the 'Eternity' scene. The walker will be invited to join the group.

any country that has brought up a whole generation on nationalism and anti-Semitism avoid those poisons seeping into the population?[19]

This letter is a very angry document indeed, hand-written and dashed off at speed, yet nevertheless carefully photocopied before posting. It is important, since it demonstrates that anti-Semitism was far from over with the death of Stalin, but instead dogged Norstein throughout his life. Its catalogue of examples includes a direct quote from a previous head of the animation studio using racist language almost unbelievable from a person in his position, and ends with a post-script apologising for going on at such length: 'This letter didn't turn out to be brief after all. You can be brief within the pale of settlement. You don't need to explain anything there.'[20] The pale of settlement was the ghetto area to which Jews had been confined under the Tsars. Bitter words, then.

There are more, in an interview in *Iskusstvo kino*'s issue focusing on religion, produced at the end of 2000 to mark the jubilee of Christianity. The Jewish Norstein was initially unwilling to take part but finally agreed to do so, speaking articulately about the relationship between art and

19 Letter dated 17 November 1993. Norstein no longer remembers to which newspaper it was sent.

20 Ibid.

religion. But naturally the anti-Semitism experienced during his youth cropped up.

> You couldn't take a step without someone saying you crucified Christ, and that you season your matzos with the blood of murdered babies. It was malicious old women and children who got particularly hysterical.[21]

It is hardly surprising that a childhood overshadowed by such taunts should have fostered dreams of emerging from a dark corridor into the light. In the luminous world at the end of the corridor in *Tale of Tales*, there is poetry and art, and there are eternal memories, as well as the talking cat mentioned by Norstein in his epigraph. But the element of this world that seems to share equal importance with the activities of the poet is a meal, which is provided and organised by the fisherman and his wife. A key moment, and one Norstein often mentions in conversation, is when a walker appears, a complete stranger, and is invited over in the most natural way possible to share the meal and a glass of wine. Such is the kind of world Norstein, as a child, longed for.

In 1956 Norstein's father – a machine-tool adjuster – died, at the age of 51. Norstein sees this as an indirect result of anti-Semitism, for his father had earlier been fired from his job in Moscow for no good reason, and was then forced to travel considerable distances and to work in much harsher conditions. Norstein is quite sure that this brought on the lung disease that led to his early death.

In a sense, this event marked the end of Norstein's childhood, at the age of 15. It was about this time that he began to react against the ingrained need to submit to that constant rain of insults and innuendo, though his rebellion was not aggressive. He simply ceased to see himself as a second-class citizen and formed a determination to do well despite the problems of prejudice, lack of money and lack of an educated or artistic background. He threw himself into a self-improvement campaign: painting, visiting exhibitions and reading voraciously.

21 'V pote litsa', *Iskusstvo kino* 12 (2000), p. 33.

Plate 1. 25th – the First Day, *co-directed with Arkadi Tyurin. A paean to revolutionary art. [Courtesy Films By Jove]*

Plate 2. The Fox and the Hare. *Hare and rooster prepare to do battle. [Courtesy Films By Jove]*

Plate 3 (facing page). Old woman at the stove. Yuri Norstein (1955).

Plate 4 (above). The old house in winter. Francesca Yarbusova collage for Tale of Tales.

Plate 5 (right). The old house, the poplar, the 'golden globes'. [Courtesy Films By Jove]

Plate 6 (facing page). Crows on a snow-covered tree. Yuri Norstein (1959).

Plate 7 (right). Boy shares his apple with crows – winter scene from Tale of Tales*.*
[Courtesy Films By Jove]

Plate. 8 (below). The nagging mother as seen in the film.
[Courtesy Films By Jove]

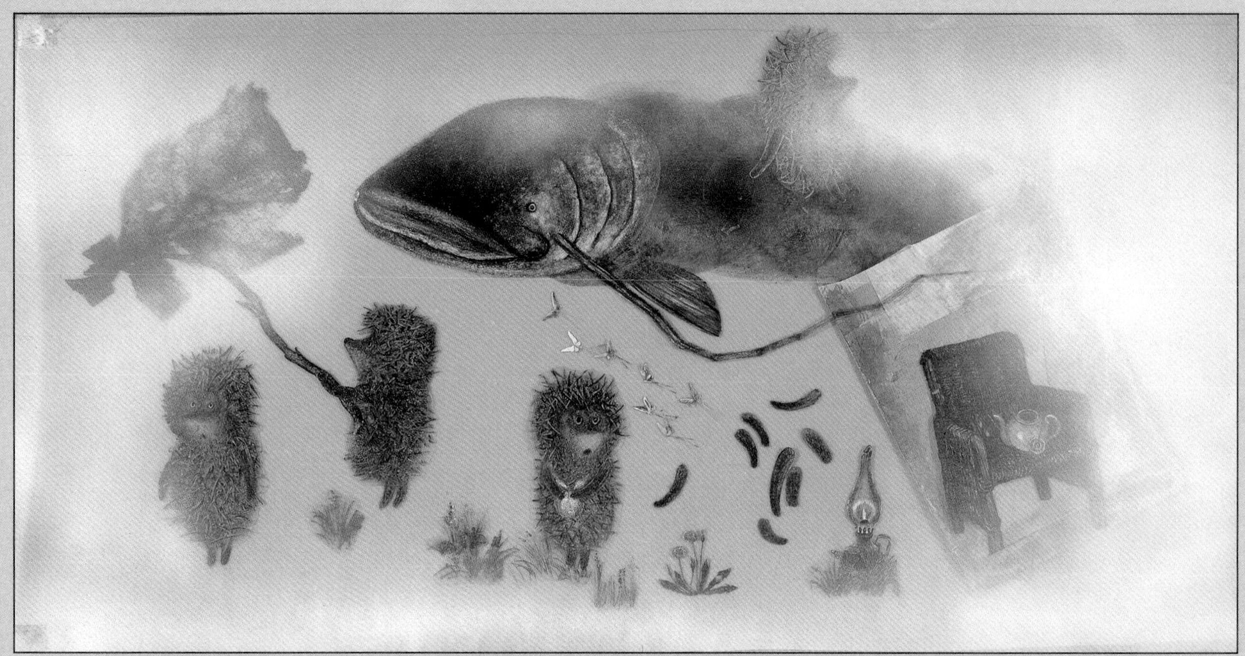

Plate 9. Repeating motifs: a giant leaf and a fish designed for use in Hedgehog in the Fog *and repeated in* Tale of Tales. *Collage by Norstein and Yarbusova.*

Plate 10. Composite sketch for Tale of Tales. *Norstein and Yarbusova.*

Plate. 11. Little Wolf collage for Tale of Tales*. Norstein and Yarbusova.*

Plate. 12. Two sketches for the 'Eternity' sequence. Unusually, these were done by Norstein and not by Yarbusova.

Plate. 13. Valentin Olshvang's design sketch for Good Night Kids *title sequence.*

3

Light rooms, high windows …

The creative world opening up 1956-1967

Not only for the 15 year-old Norstein, but also for the country as a whole, 1956 was a decisive year. Khrushchev had been in power since Stalin's death in 1953, but repressive domestic policies had been loosening up only very gradually.[22] In 1956, however, the 20th Party Congress took place, Khrushchev's first – and he took the opportunity to deliver a resounding condemnation of Stalin. It was the first time anyone had dared do so. This event was to transform Soviet cultural life for several years to come, and it was against this more liberal background that Norstein was now determinedly forging his way in the world of art and literature.

This period marked definite progress along the dark corridor from Maryina Roshcha to the world of the arts, basking in luminescence – but it must not be assumed that his life had been all darkness and barbarity until that time. A neighbour, for example, had inspired the boy at an early age:

> [There was] one very cultured lady – she had travelled all over Europe in her youth, before the First World War. She had pictures on the walls, her own paintings of Venice, for example. Little watercolours. It made a great impression – my first glimpse into a different world. This was much more important than just reading books and going to art galleries.[23]

But books were important too, and someone, spotting the boy's interest, had given him a book of reproductions of Russian painters. The 7 year-old had shown a healthy interest in Alexander Ivanov's *Head of John the Baptist* and a (perhaps at that age no more than dutiful) admiration for Russia's greatest medieval icon-painter, Andrei Rublev. But, interestingly, he had already conceived a fascination for the early nineteenth-century genre painter, Pavel Fedotov. A key influence on the later nineteenth-century Realists including Repin, and himself much influenced by Hogarth, Fedotov was a merciless satirist of contemporary society. The young Norstein was particularly attached to one of Fedotov's later paintings, *Encore, Again, Encore* (*Encore, yeshche, encore*), showing a bored officer extending a stick for his poodle to jump over. The poodle has obviously jumped,

22 Ilya Ehrenburg's 1954 *The Thaw* (*Ottepel*) was, however, indicative of slightly more liberal times and gave its name to the more open period to come.

23 Interview with Yuri Norstein, 12 April 2000, Moscow.

Fig. 16. Light days: Norstein's art school in Krasnopresnensky as it looks today. [Photo: Yuri Norstein]

and will jump, again, again … and again.[24] The child might have been more interested in the cuteness of the poodle than the tragedy of a wasted life and of a whole social class now recognising its own irrelevance – but who can be sure? This fondness for such a critical painter could be seen as early warning of Norstein's own later appetite for subversion.

But there were not only art books. From an early age he had been devouring Jules Verne, Daniel Defoe, Jonathan Swift, H. G. Wells and the fantasy novels of Alexander Belyayev. By 12 he had moved on to Turgenev, Chekhov, Gorky and Gogol. He was particularly fond of Gogol's Romantic horror tales, which he would read by the dim, spooky light of a paraffin lamp.

Now, in 1956, the creative world really started to open up for Norstein. After the disappointment four years earlier, at the teacher training institute, Norstein was now finally able to attend a special art school for talented youngsters, two days a week, in tandem with his normal school studies. It was in an elegant old mansion in the Krasnopresnensky area of Moscow, near the planetarium. It changed his life. He calls it the beginning of his *svetlye dni*, his light days.

The drawing teacher was inspirational. Moreover, it was at this art school that he first met Edward Nazarov, now also a prominent Russian animator, and a tireless worker for the international animation community. Norstein described this period in an article commissioned by *Iskusstvo kino* in 1991 to celebrate the two men's 50th birthday:

> After the smoky communal flat with its dim light-bulb and dark corridor, the hellish sputtering of potatoes in the pan and the endless noise of clothes-washing – here were light rooms, tiled stoves with brass air-gates, high windows, revered alabaster figures of various chaps with beards… One, his hirsute face thrust forward, tortured by

24 Interview with Yuri Norstein, 12 April, 2000, Moscow.

a scream – that turned out to be Laocoön; then there was a bald one with a nose like a potato – that was Socrates; and, mutely attentive to the noise of the garden in summer, Diadumenus.

Wax vegetables and bunches of grapes with tooth-marks on them. The sweet sound of easels banging, the clinking of water-colour brushes in saucers of water. The word 'water-colour', flying, translucent, melting into the air. Conversations dying away at the appearance of the god-like Vladimir Ivanovich Apanovich. And the silence, the silence ...[25]

There Norstein drew and painted happily for two days every week. When he left school in 1958, his plan was to transfer to a full-time art college. He never aspired to do anything other than fine art, so obviously art school was the next step. But it was not to be. Entrance to art school was by examination, and Norstein failed not one but four entrance exams to various art schools. This was nothing to do with anti-Semitism. He was just hopeless at exams. Instead he ended up in a furniture factory, though still attending the Krasnopresnensky art school in the evenings.

Some cabinet-making skills must have rubbed off on Norstein, for he now makes beautiful furniture for his flat. In the factory, however, they apparently kept him in the packing case department, hammering giant nails into crates. With a career in fine arts closed to him, or certainly closed for the time being, the choice was stark: either continue hammering nails into packing cases or enter the training course of the Soyuzmultfilm animation studio. This latter option would involve trying to overcome the indifference – even disdain – he felt towards the animation he saw coming out of the studio at that time, which was all for children and modelled on Disney. It was, however, better than the packing cases, so he chose animation. It was a full-time course lasting two years, entirely practical, with excellent teachers, though the animation output he saw, with very few exceptions, continued to irritate him. Throughout the course, Norstein was nurturing the hope that this would provide him with a back-door way into a career in fine art.

Meanwhile, in the country at large, Khrushchev was gaining confidence, and both cultural and political life were becoming far more open. The Thaw influenced Norstein in two ways. Firstly, there were exhibitions to see and books to read which would certainly not have been welcomed under Stalin, and which can be seen to have had a substantial effect on his development as an artist. Yet many of the cultural events on offer, which had no direct effect at all on Norstein as an artist, nevertheless affected his personal development – as they did the whole of his generation. Unlike their fathers, whose formative years had been blighted by Stalin, this group developed a habit and a taste for independent thought. Norstein was aged 15 when the Thaw began and 22 when it ended. Even after that time, he retained the independence of thought acquired during this crucial period. Without it, he could never have made *Tale of Tales.*

One of the first big events of the Thaw and one of the most memorable for the 15 year-old Norstein was the 1956 Dresden Gallery exhibition at

25 'Vse eto bylo by smeshno ...', *Iskusstvo kino* 10 (1991), p. 136.

the Pushkin Museum of Fine Arts. This world-famous collection – of masterworks of European painting of the fifteenth to eighteenth centuries – had been moved to the Soviet Union by Russian troops in 1945. The Russian story is that the paintings, having been hidden in mines to protect them from Allied bombs, were then in danger of being blown up by Nazi soldiers retreating before the incoming Soviet troops, so the latter removed the paintings for safe keeping. The Dresden Gallery people, on the other hand, have a rather different version, with Russian 'trophy commissions', meeting to decide which works of art were worth acquiring.[26] Either way, all the greatest works ended up in the USSR and Stalin had felt no urgency about returning them to Germany. Nor, it seems, about exhibiting them in Russia. For seventeen years they remained out of public view. Under Khrushchev however it was decided to return the paintings – hence this historic exhibition, the only chance for Russians to see these treasures. Visitors, including the young Norstein and his mother, queued round the block. Some queued all night. The exhibition made an enormous impression on Norstein, and until this day it is old masters seen here whom he quotes the most in his lectures to students, and whose philosophies are carried through into his work.

To the young Norstein, walking round Moscow during this heady period, it must have seemed that the world was his oyster. Between 1956 and 1963 Russia played host to exhibitions of contemporary art from France, the UK, Belgium and America – yet these exhibitions are not even mentioned in his recollections of the time. Possibly he did visit them, but they only served to reinforce the young man's growing realisation that his interests lay elsewhere. While his contemporaries were acquiring a taste for contemporary Western culture, Norstein was discovering more in his own, Russian roots.

It was now that he discovered Tolstoy ('his unique ability to turn the essence of life inside out'[27]) and read *The Sebastopol Stories*, *The Cossacks*, *War and Peace* (many times) and his very favourite, *Hadji-Murad*. He would of course have discovered Tolstoy (and Pushkin, who was also becoming important to him at this time) with or without Khrushchev's Thaw. But not so Solzhenitsyn. The USSR, and indeed the whole world, were stunned by the publication in 1962 of Solzhenitsyn's *One Day in the Life of Ivan Denisovich* (*Odin den Ivana Denisovicha*), in the pages of the literary journal *Novy Mir*, an honest and devastatingly bleak picture of the labour camps in which, under Stalin, Soviet citizens might have found themselves on the flimsiest of pretexts. Having allowed *Ivan Denisovich*, Khrushchev then passed for publication Solzhenitsyn's *Matrena's Home* (*Matrenin dvor*) the following year – but those were the only Solzhenitsyn works of any note to be published before the beginning of *glasnost*. (Pasternak was, of course, refused publication of *Doctor Zhivago* and banned from accepting the Nobel prize offered him in 1958. So Khrushchev was far from being a steadfast supporter and promoter of openness in the arts, remaining capricious to the end.)

Norstein remembers being bowled over by both the above Solzhenitsyn works, though not by their content as much as by the beauty of the

26 Harald Marx, 'Thoughts and Observations on the Dresden Gemäldegalerie', *Masterpieces from Dresden*, Royal Academy of Arts, London 2003, p. 28.

27 Letter to the author dated 16.2.01.

writing. One might also add that their pure Russian-ness was very attractive to the filmmaker Norstein was about to become. The other major series of writings that had a profound effect on the young animator were Eisenstein's memoirs and theoretical works, which began to be released in 1964, at the very end of the Khrushchev period (they were written in the 1940s). Later in Norstein's career many would seek to analyse his work in terms of camera movement and montage (matters dealt with very specifically by Eisenstein) and compare it to that of live action directors such as Tarkovsky. Norstein always plays down any comparison of his work with live action cinema, yet it was Eisenstein – not any of the instructors at the Soyuzmultfilm animation school – who provided the young animator with his understanding of cinema. Eisenstein's theory and analysis as set out in the six published volumes, crammed with bookmarks, which are even now always to hand at the studio, taught Norstein the importance of harmony, of all elements of a film fusing into a single impetus.

The young Norstein would have had his choice of Western cinema fare, but he found very little contemporary Western cinema to his taste. Chaplin was a hero – but his work had always been available. The Thaw did however provide him with his first experience of Fellini – *Nights of Cabiria* (*Le notti di Cabiria*), *La Dolce Vita* and *La Strada*.

These influences would remain latent in Norstein, and reveal themselves at a later date (though it might well have been a later Fellini film, the autobiographical *Amarcord*, released only two years before Norstein started work on *Tale of Tales*, that provided a more immediate stimulus[28]). Suddenly the Soviet films too had become far more interesting – this was the period

Fig. 17. Grigori Chukhrai's 1959 Ballad of a Soldier.

Fig. 18. Mikhail Kalatozov's 1957 The Cranes are Flying.

28 Not only could the autobiographical nature of *Amarcord* have inspired *Tale of Tales*. Critic Mikhail Iampolski also finds *Hedgehog in the Fog* reminiscent of *Amarcord*'s fog scene: v. 'Palitra i obyektiv', *Iskusstvo kino* 2 (1980), p. 99.

Fig. 19. Sergei Bondarchuk's 1959 Destiny of a Man.

of *Ballad of a Soldier* (*Ballada o soldate*),[29] *The Cranes are Flying* (*Letyat zhuravli*)[30] and *Destiny of a Man* (*Sudba cheloveka*).[31] Admittedly, these dealt with tried and tested war themes – but unlike their Socialist Realist predecessors they portrayed, honestly and movingly, real individuals with real weaknesses. This was completely unheard of in Soviet cinema. Perhaps closest to Norstein's heart was Marlen Khutsiyev's *I Am Twenty* (*Mne dvadtsat let*), which was also made just after this period, though not released until 1965

29 Grigori Chukhrai, 1959.

30 Mikhail Kalatozov, 1957.

31 Sergei Bondarchuk, 1959.

Fig. 20. The massive façade of the Soyuzmultfilm drawn animation studio. [Photo Clare Kitson]

(and even then in a severely cut form). This was obviously a little too honest for the authorities as it dealt with the confusions of Norstein's (exact) contemporaries at a moment of changing ideals and aspirations.

As well as Russian art and literature, Norstein began at this time to take an interest in the poetry of other cultures. From the age of 15, this included Japanese poetry – tanka and haiku – which was to lead to a wide interest in oriental art and philosophy, evident later in his films. Norstein's first contact with Japanese poetry produced what we would call a meeting of minds though Norstein, far more appropriately, calls it a 'fusion of souls'. He was captivated by its somehow undefined quality – it was not cut-and-dried like its European counterparts. When he took up animation he discovered that Japanese principles – philosophical and religious, relating to space, to objects, to nature, to death – were rather more relevant to his work than those he had been brought up with.

In 1961 the two-year animation course came to an end and no way of forging a fine art career had as yet presented itself. The unwilling animator therefore found himself an employee of the giant Soyuzmultfilm Moscow animation studio, working firstly in the drawn animation studio which lay behind the monumental frontage of 23a Kalyayevskaya (now re-named Dolgorukovskaya) Street, and subsequently in the beautiful converted church in the Arbat which housed the puppet studio.

Twenty-seven years later, Norstein was to write a letter of resignation to the director of the studio, accusing the management of 'elementary carelessness and negligence' and speaking of a 'loss of all criteria', 'mutual suspicion' and 'pathological jealousy'. 'The whole studio', he said, 'is careering downhill like a train without a driver … '. [32]

Yet, when Norstein joined the studio during the final, heady days of Khrushchev's Thaw, it had not seemed so bad. After the constant diet of children and Disney look-alikes, things were beginning to liven up. First there were the rumours: 'Fedka Khitruk does things differently.'[33] And he

32 Letter to E.V. Stachenkov, undated but written on or shortly before 8.8.1989. Unpublished, but extracts quoted in 'Kinostudiya "Soyuzmultfilm" segodnya', A. M. Orlov, on www.aha.ru.

33 Yuri Norstein, 'Priznaniye masteru', *Iskusstvo kino* 8 (1987), p. 74.

Fig. 21. Once a disused church housing a bustling puppet animation studio. Now, lavishly restored, a church again. [Photo Clare Kitson]

did. For a start, he would only accept youngsters into the team for his debut film, *The Story of One Crime* (*Istoriya odnogo prestupleniya,* 1962) – though not Norstein, who envied his colleagues Nazarov, Nosyrev and Petrov that opportunity. It was the first time Soviet animation had touched on social problems (the plot trigger being noise pollution in overcrowded living conditions) and it actually caused great indignation among Party loyalists, who saw it as a criticism of government housing policy. It was a completely different approach to animation, with an ironic, adult world-view, done in a pared-down style totally divorced from the rounded Disney-esque forms previously dominating Soviet animation. But for Norstein, 'even this event didn't change anything as far as I was concerned.'[34]

It did, however, stimulate other animators in the studio and gradually

34 Interview with Yuri Norstein, 12 April 2000, Moscow.

Fig. 22. Fedor Khitruk's The Story of One Crime.
[Courtesy Films By Jove]

in the late 1960s a new genre of adult animation came into existence – though it was of course tiny in comparison with the production of children's films.

In the outside world, meanwhile, a group of contemporary artists were also hoping to benefit from the new freedoms. In December 1962 they mounted a historic, and notorious, exhibition at the Manège (Moscow's main exhibition hall) celebrating 30 years of MOSKh, the Moscow grouping of the Union of Soviet Artists. This exhibition of highly experimental work represented the high point of the opposition to Socialist Realism, and it became too much for the USSR Academy of Arts, the guardians of socialist ideology in art. They persuaded the not-very-culturally-aware Khrushchev to visit the exhibition which, not surprisingly, he did not like. This was the beginning of the end for the Thaw in Soviet culture. Many of the best avant-garde talents were completely shut out of official cultural life and forced to go underground. This included the sculptor Ernst Neizvestny, who was at the time particularly loathed by Khrushchev, thanks to the efforts of the Academy. (Though there may have been a subsequent rapprochement, since on Khrushchev's death it was none other than Neizvestny who was commissioned to sculpt a massive abstract memorial to adorn his grave.)

By late 1963 there was a new ideological clampdown and by 1964 Khrushchev, grown increasingly unpredictable, had been replaced by Brezhnev, at first in a triumvirate with Kosygin and Podgorny. Fortunately, this team had other things on their minds than the activities of the animators at Soyuzmultfilm. In this hive of activity (then turning out about forty films a year) spirits were still high, excepting the new recruit, Norstein. He was obliged to spend time in all sections of the studio – starting in the drawn animation studio, then moving to the puppet section, which included cut-outs – animating for other people, sometimes for his contemporaries who had been promoted ahead of him. In the course of forty or so films as animator he became a consummate craftsman in all three techniques, which probably helps to explain the extraordinary technical ingenuity later manifested in *Tale of Tales*. It was, however, a frustrating time, working on many 'uninspiring films by other directors. I quite often spoke my mind about their poor quality. I hated myself, the films, the studio.'[35] The first of these uninspiring works, incidentally, had been *Living Numbers* (*Zhivye tsifry*, 1962), a paean to Khrushchev's 20-year plan for the building of Communism, on which he animated musical vignettes extolling Soviet progress in chemistry, construction, etc. Norstein's lack of enthusiasm was mirrored by that of the film's director, Roman Davydov, whose report on the first-timer noted that he was 'very disorganised'.[36]

It was to be another five years before Norstein was able to work as a director (with Arkadi Tyurin) on his own film and fourteen before he was given the official designation 'director', though by that time he would actually have directed several films. Norstein claims that, of a group of similarly-gifted graduates from the two-year course, his own promotion came many years after the other graduates', despite the fact that the veteran and greatly revered director Ivan Ivanov-Vano was constantly interceding on his behalf. Norstein sees this as proof of anti-Semitism, and there was certainly an element of this, though one wonders whether this aspiring painter might also have managed to alienate his bosses by his continuing, unconcealed disdain for the bulk of animation produced at the studio.

Ivanov-Vano, however, was indeed a source of unfailing support for Norstein. He was also responsible for some of the more interesting projects Norstein was able to work on as animator and, later, co-director. One of the more notable cut-out films was Ivanov-Vano's 1964 *The Left-Handed Craftsman* (*Levsha*, also known in English translation as *The Steel Flea*, based on the 1881 satire by Nikolai Leskov), a project which appealed to Norstein's taste for Russian classic literature.

He found himself working on that film with Arkadi Tyurin, with whom he was later to co-direct *25th – the First Day* (*25*e *– pervy den*). Tyurin remembers well Norstein's ingenuity in manipulating the cut-outs. Cut-out animation differs in one major aspect from traditional cel animation. In the latter technique, images are re-drawn on celluloid, with small differences to give the impression of movement, and later, when a section is complete, the images are photographed one at a time. In cut-out animation, however, the images are not on large sheets of celluloid, but are cut out into the required shapes for sections of the characters' bodies. Rather than being re-drawn, these forms are actually, physically, moved, on a horizontal table under the camera, one frame being shot after each move. As in most cut-out films, *The Left-Handed Craftsman*'s characters were made with beautifully engineered hinges holding the bodies together while allowing adequate movement at the joints. With a mixture of amusement and terror the crew one day observed Norstein tearing the hinges off all the cut-outs. His hunch that these hinges were impeding the free and

35 Letter to the author, 20 April 2001.

36 In Norstein's personal file at the studio. Unpublished.

Fig. 23. The Left-Handed Craftsman, *directed by Ivan Ivanov-Vano. [Courtesy Films By Jove]*

natural movement of the characters turned out to be absolutely correct and was later vindicated in his own work as director. (He now uses hinges very rarely indeed – when, for example, he needs a hare's ears to flap as he walks, or a bird's thin neck to remain flexible.)

Having earlier failed to get himself into the crew of Khitruk's *Story of One Crime*, Norstein now managed to work for Khitruk on the 1965 *Bonifacio's Holiday* (*Kanikuly Bonifatsiya*). He also worked on some of the most beautiful of the studio's puppet films, including Vadim Kurchevsky's poetic *My Green Crocodile* (*Moi zeleny krokodil*, 1966), in which the eponymous reptile falls for an elegant white cow, and Roman Kachanov's *The Mitten* (*Varezhka,* 1967), a moving story about a lonely child. Yet filled as he was with admiration for these directors, Norstein at this stage conceived a dislike for the very principle of puppet animation. As with cut-outs, puppet animation is a stop-motion technique. In this case the camera set-up is similar to live-action, facing the puppets from the side rather than from above. Thanks to the puppets' either flexible or jointed internal skeleton, they can be moved almost imperceptibly between single shots. But the aim – and this was especially the case in Soviet puppet animation – was to ape live action, an ambition Norstein heartily disapproves of.

In the late 1960s, it became obvious that Brezhnev was no liberal-inclined Khrushchev, but neither was he a Stalin. There was none of the unpredictability of the Khrushchev era, and no mass arrests as in Stalin's time. Brezhnev's way of dealing with undesirable influences in the arts was simple: authors and artists he did not like, both Western and Russian, were either not published/exhibited at all or so minimally as to render them almost invisible. And, more to the point, this deprived out-of-favour Soviet artists of any means of earning a living. Very few dissidents were imprisoned, but some were still being sent to psychiatric hospitals and many were given dreary tasks intended to blunt their creative edge.

Norstein characterises the period:

> In one word – it was stuffy. We didn't have enough air. But the strange thing is that when a lot of things outside you are closed off you go inside yourself and find the freedom you need. [37]

And indeed artists, writers and filmmakers – and readers and cinemagoers – were manifesting an extraordinary 'inner freedom'. There was enormous creative activity during the Brezhnev years and an audience hungry for good new work. The coincidence of a highly educated population with the lack of easily-available stimulation increased this hunger.

Throughout the 1960s and 1970s subversive novels were written 'for the desk drawer', i.e. in the knowledge that they were unlikely to get published in the climate of the time. Yet some did get published – it was a bit of a lottery – and there was a lively market in *samizdat* (privately published, unauthorised) literature.

Cinema activity was also pushing the boundaries of what was considered acceptable by the regime. This is quite remarkable considering the quantities of state funding that were poured into each feature film – unlike the writing of a novel – and the way the film industry was structured. The State Cinema Authority – Goskino – checked all scripts before authorising filmmakers to proceed and there was a network of KGB representatives at the studios, many under the guise of so-called 'redactors', who supposedly had some sort of script-editing role. Yet, even so, challenging and even subversive films got made. Tarkovsky is a prime example of this. Natasha Synessios points out[38] that he managed to persuade the atheist Soviet state to fund a film about an icon-painter monk (*Andrei Rublev*, completed 1966) and another, *Mirror* (*Zerkalo*, 1974), about conscience and memory, on the basis of a proposal which frankly acknowledged that the director had no idea at that stage of the film's ending and ultimate structure. His films systematically disregarded the predominant ideology and he regularly changed his authorised scripts during filming. Yet, despite maybe understandable 'delays' of a year or two in release, none of his films was actually banned for the duration.

Other filmmakers were not so lucky. Their films ended up on the

37 Interview with Yuri Norstein, 15 April 2000, Moscow.

38 In a lecture entitled 'Art and Censorship: Tarkovsky at Mosfilm', given at a conference in Athens, 7–8 December 2002 (unpublished).

Fig. 24. Andrei Tarkovsky's 1966 Andrei Rublev.

censor's shelf, only to reappear when the *glasnost*-era Filmmakers' Union created a Conflict Commission to sort out exactly what was on those shelves and to get the good films into the cinema. But the important thing is that they were *made*.

In the animation area, however, things were rather different. Though the animation studios existed within exactly the same framework – reporting to Goskino, with Goskino checking script suitability and with a similar network of informers – the atmosphere was rather more relaxed. For one thing, animation had rarely dealt with contemporary, recognisable life – in fact it rarely even dealt with human characters. Secondly, the major animation studio, Soyuzmultfilm in Moscow, where Norstein and the other best-known Soviet animators were working, seemed to suffer less than most from the stifling influence of the KGB 'redactors'. One of its script editors, in fact, Natasha Abramova, who was to work on *Tale of Tales*, was an energetic puller of wool over Goskino's eyes. And, finally, nobody seemed to take animation very seriously. It was always assumed that these were light-hearted comedies for a family audience. So the scripts were perhaps scrutinised less rigorously and when films were completed they were far less likely to be shelved than were their live action feature counterparts.

In the general climate of creativity and defiance, the animators at Soyuzmultfilm became fairly adventurous. The only animated film ever to be totally banned (until *perestroika*) was Andrei Khrzhanovsky's 1968 *The Glass Harmonica (Steklyannaya garmonika)*. This is the tale of a mythical city run by a ruthless band of bureaucrats, which is visited by a musician playing a glass harmonica (a beautiful instrument consisting of glass cylinders of varying dimensions). He proceeds to demonstrate the powerful effect art can have on the deformations of a totalitarian state. The bureaucrats did, in truth, look like Communist authority figures, but Khrzhanovsky had

Fig. 25. Andrei Khrzhanovsky's banned film, The Glass Harmonica. *[Courtesy Films By Jove]*

tried to guard against the authorities themselves jumping to this conclusion by adding an epigraph to the film explaining that this nasty crowd were in fact evil capitalists. This was all to no avail, however, and the film was banned until the great unshelving of the *glasnost* period.

Some other films should perhaps have been taken more seriously by Goskino, but instead they slipped through unnoticed. Khrzhanovsky's own earlier *Once There Was a Man Called Kozyavin* (*Zhil-byl Kozyavin,* 1966) is a

Fig. 26. Andrei Khrzhanovsky's Once There Was a Man Called Kozyavin. *[Courtesy Films By Jove]*

Fig. 27. Norstein's drawing of Francesca, 1968.

devastating and very funny satire about a bureaucrat's lack of imagination and, frankly, brains. Fedor Khitruk's *Man in the Frame (Chelovek v ramke)*, of the same year, tells the tale of a coward (a bureaucrat, a Party man almost certainly), fearful of stepping out of the picture frame that surrounds him. As the years pass the man remains insignificant but the frame grows more and more solid, finally concealing him completely.

Such were Norstein's role models during the long period of his enforced wait for director status. Things were changing in animation and there was a willingness both to address new, adult subjects and to experiment with new aesthetics. But there was another important influence at the studio at that time, in the person of a final year design student from the All-Union State Institute of Cinematography (VGIK), who used to come into the studio in the evenings to help out on some of the design work. Francesca Yarbusova was, like Norstein, an unwilling recruit to animation, having wanted to design live action films. It had been that same *éminence grise*, Ivan Ivanov-Vano (who was teaching at VGIK as well as directing at the studio), who had told her that as a girl she would never manage to order tough carpenters around on the set and she would be much better off in animation, where she could keep everything under her control. Little did she know …

When the highly talented Yarbusova graduated from VGIK (as an animation designer) in 1967 she, as a native Muscovite, was relieved to be allocated to Soyuzmultfilm. (There was no question of graduating students choosing where they wanted to work – she could have been sent anywhere in the country.) That same year she and Norstein married, initiating a personal and professional partnership which has been creatively unique (she has designed all Norstein's films), if tumultuous.

Norstein was still at this time living with his mother in one room of the communal flat, but by the 1960s the accommodation did not seem right for a married couple. Thus, finally, in 1967 at the age of 26, Norstein left Maryina Roshcha, the scene of his post-war childhood.

Artwork by Francesca Yarbusova

Plate 14. The hare and the wolf. Sketch for The Fox and the Hare.

Plate 15. The hare and the rooster. Sketch for The Fox and the Hare.

Plate 16 (above). In the pergola. Sketch for The Heron and the Crane.

Plate 17 (left). Hedgehog and owl. Sketch for Hedgehog in the Fog.

Plate 18 (above). Composite sketch for Tale of Tales.

Plate 19 (right). Little Wolf at the door of the old house. Sketch for Tale of Tales.

Plate 20. Midday. Maquette for Tale of Tales.

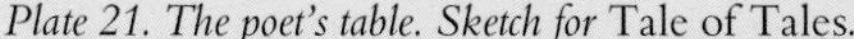

Plate 21. The poet's table. Sketch for Tale of Tales.

Plate 22 (above). The bird's funeral. Sketch for unfilmed scene of Tale of Tales.

Plate 23 (right). Francesca Yarbusova in 1997.
[Photo Yuri Norstein]

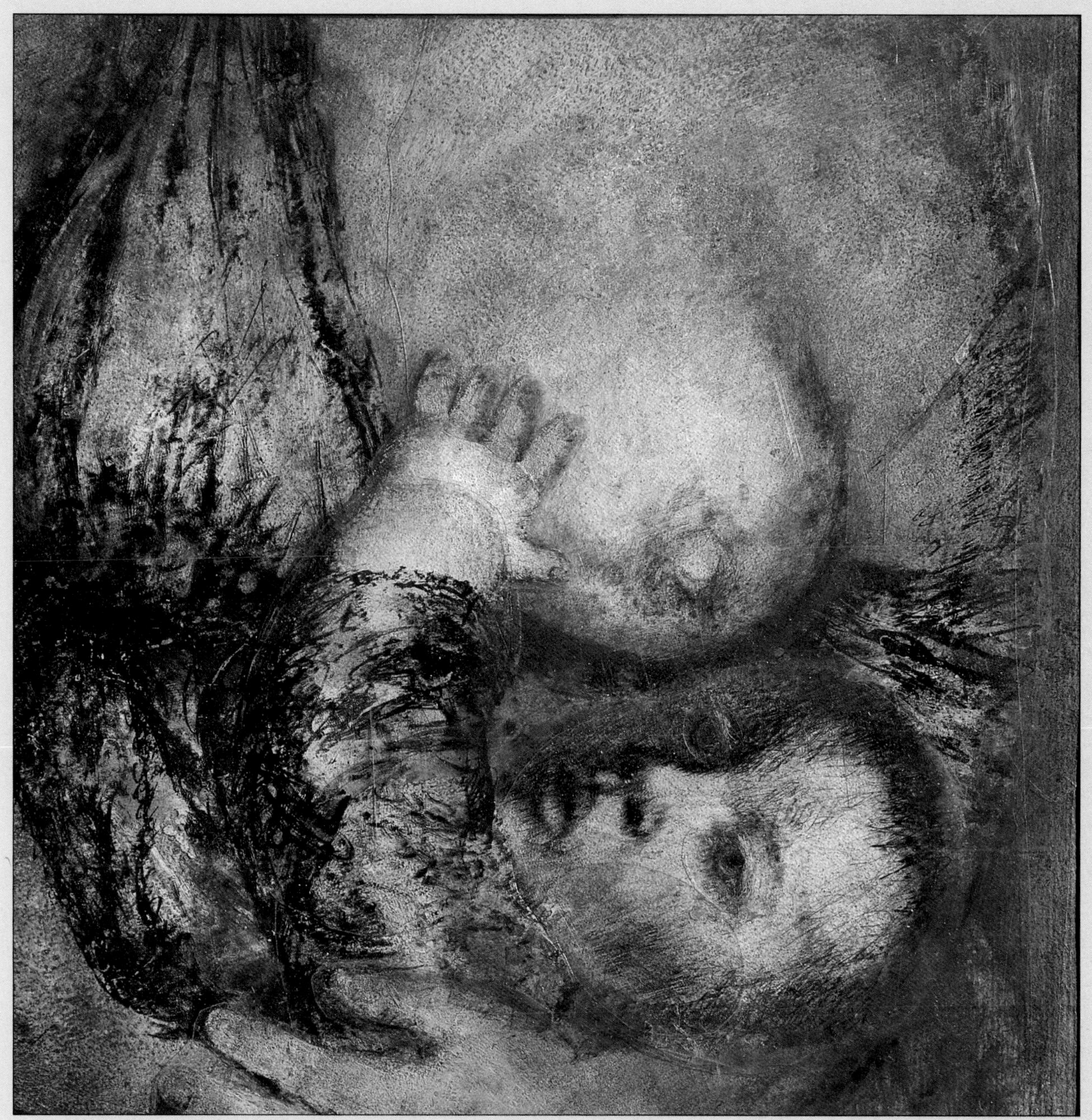

Plate 24. Baby at breast. Son Borya's face was the model. Francesca Yarbusova collage for Tale of Tales.

Plate 25. Sketch for The Overcoat.

4

A mix of micro-histories …

The elements coalesce 1967-1976

Just as 1956 had been a fateful year for Norstein, 1967 was to prove equally so. The move away from Maryina Roshcha would trigger a series of reflections about childhood, family life and community, which would become an unquenchable urge to make a film on those themes. His marriage to Yarbusova in the same year was very soon to produce two children, who cannot but have affected Norstein's view of childhood, and that marriage would also become the most important working partnership of his career. This was also the year in which he met the other woman who would make such a profound contribution to *Tale of Tales*, the (at that time) banned playwright and novelist, Lyudmila Petrushevskaya. It was also, finally, the year in which Norstein at long last began work on his first film as director, or rather co-director, together with designer Arkadi Tyurin.

Perhaps it was also about this time that the Brezhnev-era 'stuffiness', the lack of creative air so lamented by Norstein and his peers, began to pervade the studio. For it would gradually become obvious that apart from Norstein, who would come to maturity as a director in the 1970s, and Khrzhanovsky, who continued to experiment, this decade would be less innovative than the 1960s. Khitruk, who had done so much to inspire the younger animators, continued to make excellent films, but he never bettered his creative spurt of the previous decade. Other directors were using exquisite design, notably Anatoly Petrov, whose unique look seemed to hover somewhere between Socialist Realism and Pop Art (especially in *Polygon*, his sci-fi fantasy peopled by well-known stars of Hollywood and European cinema). Few, however, were interested in experimenting with innovative content, narrative or animation techniques.

Whether or not this period did in fact mark a clamping down by studio bosses, it was certainly now that Norstein had his first major clash with authority, and this was to affect his future attitude on censorship and compromise. It may not be too fanciful to see here the origin of Norstein's disdain for philistinism, which was the main thrust of all the *Tale of Tales* scripts. (Only in the final film did this theme recede somewhat, though traces do remain.)

The film in question was *25th – the First Day*, a paean to the art of the October Revolution [see colour plate no. 1]. By 1967 Soviet citizens knew about Stalin's atrocities, but nothing of those of the early Bolsheviks. Lenin was still a hero and Norstein and Tyurin's revolutionary fervour was genuine. The film's title was from a Mayakovsky poem[39] and the images were taken from Soviet art of the 1910s and 20s, including Tatlin, Petrov-Vodkin, Chagall, Malevich, Deineka and the graphic work of Mayakovsky, among others. The spirit of Braque is there too, in an almost Cubist use of multiple viewpoints in a single, flat image. The music is by Shostakovich.

There were, however, ructions behind the scenes, which made this film particularly important in forming Norstein's attitude to authority. He had always admired the avant-garde art of this period, this extraordinary attempt to convey the spirit of the times in state-sponsored art. He and Tyurin were inspired by these artists' idea of a 'regenerated world, a destiny shaped by the people themselves.'[40] However, it was hard to get hold of some of this work, for certain artists had been out of favour for decades. Pavel Filonov, specifically, had been banned on the eve of his one-man show in 1930 and his work would not be seen again in public until the early 1980s. Filonov's ostracisation was perhaps not surprising. His work was governed by theoretical beliefs that were unique among his peers and for which he coined the terms Universal Flowering and Analytical Art. His system involved pictorial analysis of particular details and their reproduction in an organic fashion, simulating processes in nature, to cover whole canvases with 'atoms' of delicate detail. The result was a mosaic that could certainly be seen as 'formalist', sometimes even abstract. Despite Filonov's bad odour with the authorities – or, who knows, perhaps that made him seem all the more attractive – Norstein and Tyurin wanted to base the film's structure on Filonov's principles of composition and actually to use a Filonov work, *Formula for Revolution* (*Formula revolyutsii*), in the film's finale. The finale idea was, of course, vetoed. However, the directors did manage to retain a Filonov-inspired, semi-abstract freedom of approach to form, and to carry into the film the painter's dynamic, very cinematic feel for the movement of crowds impelled by revolutionary zeal.

The directors were also told there could be no film about the revolution without Lenin – so Norstein and Tyurin turned to the work of Vladimir Favorsky, a highly respected teacher at the Higher Artistic-Technical Workshops (VKhUTEMAS), which had done much to foster revolutionary art in the 1920s. They blew up an engraving by Favorsky, *Lenin and the Revolution* (*Lenin i revolyutsiya*), cut out the figure of Lenin and animated it, giving the effect of a documentary shot. That was also vetoed and the scene cut. As first-time directors, Norstein and Tyurin were finally forced to acquiesce with the authorities' suggestion and end the film with some Lenin footage culled from a revolutionary poster that Norstein characterises as 'monstrous'. Even so, the film was officially disliked and criticised as degenerate. 'That was my compromise,' Norstein comments. 'But when I realised what I'd done, I vowed that, as a director, I'd never compromise again to the detriment of a film.'[41]

After this *débâcle* it was perhaps not surprising that Norstein was not

39 'Vladimir Ilyich Lenin', 1924.

40 Interview with Yuri Norstein by Films By Jove, January 2001, Moscow.

41 Interview with Yuri Norstein, 12 April 2000, Moscow.

Fig. 28. Battle by the Kerzhenets, *co-directed by Ivan Ivanov-Vano and Norstein.*
[Courtesy Films By Jove]

immediately granted official director status. In 1969, however, and even without the official status, Norstein was allocated a film to direct. This little-known addition to the Norstein oeuvre, *Children and Matches* (*Deti i spichki*), got me very excited when I heard about it, only to have its director pour cold water on my enthusiasm. It turns out to be a cut-out fire safety film for children, dashed off to an exceedingly tight deadline with no scope for directorial innovation and, according to Norstein, 'complete rubbish'. Perhaps it was his punishment for *25th*.

But again Ivanov-Vano was ready to offer support and some more interesting films to work on. The first of these was as assistant director on *The Seasons* (*Vremena goda,* 1969), a puppet-animated evocation of the seasons set to Tchaikovsky's cycle of short keyboard pieces. This was in no way experimental, and Norstein was, as we know, not a fan of puppets. The design, however, was rooted in Russian folk-art, which was very much to his taste.

Battle by the Kerzhenets (*Secha pri Kerzhentse,* 1971), this one co-directed with Ivanov-Vano, was a far more significant piece of work, and of more importance in Norstein's development. In this film, Russian icons, miniatures and frescoes of the 14th to 16th centuries were animated to Rimsky-Korsakov's *Legend of the Invisible City of Kitezh (Skazaniye o nevidimom grade Kitezhe i deve Fevronii)*. Norstein was responsible for all technical aspects, Tyurin was again in the group, as co-art director, and Yarbusova also worked in the design department – her first project together with her husband. Though the design was based on Byzantine art, Norstein again introduced elements from Russia's post-revolutionary flowering. This time it is Malevich, whose painting *Red Cavalry* is borrowed in the scene where the Tatar cavalry storms across the steppes to meet the Russian defenders.[42] Norstein:

> That film was very important to me. It gave me a sense of the resonance, the musicality of forms, the musicality of action. This is nothing to do with the superficial musical rhythm, but a feeling for internal structure.[43]

The film went on to win the Grand Prix at the Zagreb Animation Festival.

Norstein's 'workbook' (something like a car's service book, recording career developments throughout one's working life) shows his promotions (and hence pay-rises) progressing at a snail's pace. Yet in 1972, while still officially a humble 'animator category 1', he was commissioned to make his first fully independent film as director. By this time, the unwilling animator had had something of a change of heart and was now passionately aspiring to *direct* animation – partly out of frustration with some of the bad projects he had been forced to animate but also, interestingly, because his desire to immerse himself in painting had waned. Perhaps animation, at this stage, seemed to demand a lesser degree of personal commitment. Now, in 1972, an Italian producer was co-ordinating a group of European folk tales, and Norstein was nominated to direct the Soviet Union's contribution, *The Fox and the Hare* (*Lisa i zayats*), a tale from Russian folklore, with design oriented towards folk-art style [see colour plate no. 2]. Specific inspiration came, apparently, from the old spinning wheels on display in the ethnographic museum, which not only featured carved images telling traditional tales but even displayed them in successive frames, much like an animation storyboard. Norstein recalls, incidentally, that this design decision provoked violent disagreements with his designer wife – a foretaste of fireworks to come.[44]

It was when Fedor Khitruk first saw this film that he really understood what an unusual talent the studio was nurturing in the person of Norstein:

> We weren't expecting too much innovation in this film. It was traditional material, of the kind we have been animating since time immemorial … We all knew exactly how you could film that sort of

42 'Norstein on Norstein and Russian Animation', interview by Stanislav Ulver in *Asifa News* vol. 13, 1(2000), p. 7.

43 Interview with Yuri Norstein, 12 April 2000, Moscow.

44 'Norstein on Norstein and Russian Animation', p. 8.

Fig. 29. Two disputatious birds. The Heron and the Crane. *[Courtesy Films By Jove]*

> story, and we thought Norstein would do it tastefully, with talent and with some sweet, witty touches ...
>
> The young director's film turned out to be a real surprise – and not only to me. He amazed us. It was strikingly original in form. The film frame was emphasised by the presence of a wooden frame, like a window looking into an unknown world. There was a new texture, a new system that made the characters 'act' ... There was no detail in the movement, no smoothness, no delicacy in the gestures. Yet despite this the director managed to create extraordinarily expressive, psychologically accurate characters ... He did this firstly by his portrayal of the characters and secondly by the design of the surroundings. The openly decorative and elegantly stylised landscape [...] creates the right emotional atmosphere and pulls us into this world born of the artist's imagination ...[45]

But, successful as *The Fox and the Hare* undoubtedly was, most critics agree that Norstein's next film, *The Heron and the Crane* (*Tsaplya i zhuravl*, 1974), was even better. It is the story of two lonely birds desperately wanting to get together, but unable to overcome the barrier of their differently-shaped necks. Khitruk again:

45 *Detskaya literatura*, April 1977, pp. 67–68, quoted in *Soyuzmultfilm*, Soyuzinformkino, Moscow 1981, p. 31.

> The comic tale of two disputatious and wilful individuals became, in Norstein's hands, a sad story about loneliness. To me it's pure Chekhov – about happiness that never was, about how two absurd and unhappy people, trying to stand up for themselves, destroy their own lives.[46]

Norstein himself relates the plot to a Gogol story in which an old couple realise they have wasted their whole lives pursuing utterly trivial antagonisms.[47] Yet despite these depths, *The Heron and the Crane* remains a children's film, packed with delightful comic detail. It is also a film in which the landscape plays a major part – it becomes a 'third character', as Khitruk puts it.

The voice of Innokenti Smoktunovsky – perhaps best known in the West as Kozintsev's Hamlet, but well known in Russia for his stage roles including much Chekhov – produced a narration perfectly in tune with the mood of the film.

The partnership with Yarbusova was crucial to the success of *Heron*, which used a technique they had developed to a certain extent with *The Fox and the Hare*. Norstein and Yarbusova always work with cut-outs rather than traditional re-drawn animation, and in their early work the figures had been cut out in the normal way from card. But in *The Fox and the Hare* they had experimented by creating the cut-out limbs of the bear character from celluloid, drawing the bear on the cel but leaving clear celluloid around the edge so as to give an impression of drawn rather than cut-out animation. Now, with *Heron*, they perfected this technique. Here everything was done on cel, cut out to shape. They now covered the cel edges with black paint so that these would not reflect light and would thus remain invisible, and added various kinds of textures to the surface. Furthermore, characters and even elements of the background tended to consist of more than one layer of textured cel. The Greek columns, for example, consisted of cut-out cel with grey paper stuck underneath and texturing on top.

There was a firm policy decision taken not to use normal flat, painted backgrounds:

> Big things, separate from the characters? No. Francesca and I hold to a principle not to draw backgrounds like that, in a single layer. We build them up. […] The house in *Tale of Tales*, for example, is made of about ten layers. There's the house, then more layers of cel with texture on them. And then you draw a few details on the last one. Then the layers play off each other and you get an element of improvisation that's full of creative energy. If you take away one layer of cel you lose the depth. I call it *lisserovki* [fine artists call it 'scumble' in English], after the painting method. Rembrandt or Veronese would do a preliminary texture, for the folds in draperies for example, with a layer of thick paint in a mixture of white, umber and sepia and then when that was dry add a layer of colour mixed with varnish. They'd vary the colour of the texture and of the translucent layer on top to produce an endless variety. Because of the depth of the translucent layer it acts as a lens. […] So it's the same with our backgrounds. It's

46 Ibid.

47 'Old-World Landowners' ('Starosvetskiye pomeshchiki'), part of the *Mirgorod* cycle, 1835.

> an absolutely classical principle in painting, the layering of one texture on another.
>
> And it was Francesca and I who discovered how to do this in animation. No one else uses it. At Soyuzmultfilm they always did backgrounds, beautifully done, professional, but they always looked dead to me.
>
> But with our method even the thickness of the backgrounds plays its part. [...] If you painted the same thing on a flat surface you wouldn't get the same optical effect. And also, when we get a complex background and then a texture one level above it [on the multiplane animation stand, discussed below], then you get a play of the air, of the space. I love that, and Francesca does it perfectly.[48]

In *The Heron and the Crane* the technique is perhaps not yet used to its full potential, but nevertheless it is noticeable that, as Khitruk observes, the background does come alive and participate in the film to a much greater extent than those 'dead' backgrounds Norstein so disliked in the studio.

Just as crucial as these design developments were the innovations worked out during this period in the camera department, with the much-loved and much-missed cameraman on Norstein's early films, the late Alexander Zhukovsky. Norstein considered him a cinematographic genius: 'He humanised space. [...] He did not merely *film*. He influenced the light, the film stock, the camera, the drawings with his entire being.'[49] It was with Zhukovsky that Norstein developed his unique multiplane animation stand, the prototype of which was first used on *The Heron and the Crane*.

Multiplane animation was not a new idea. Animators had been striving since the beginning for a means of adding depth to the two-dimensional animated image. Lotte Reiniger had used a very simple multiplane system for her 1926 *Adventures of Prince Achmed* (*Die Abenteuer des Prinzen Achmed*). The Fleischer studio version, patented in 1934, was far more elaborate, consisting of a three-dimensional background set constructed on a turntable. A single-frame camera was set up next to this (looking horizontally at the set, as for live action) and cels were mounted vertically in front of the camera, which were replaced in the normal way between shots, while at the same time the turntable was rotated. Thus two-dimensional characters appeared to be walking through a three-dimensional set.

Ub Iwerks developed a more practical system, followed by Disney, the latter using the system to change the face of Hollywood animation. It was based on a traditional animation camera, looking downwards onto a stand, which supported several independently mobile sheets of glass, each holding cels featuring the action taking place at the different levels from foreground to background, with the very bottom sheet holding any painted backgrounds or, sometimes, simply skies. It could achieve the most sophisticated effects, for example scenes in which the camera appears to be panning laterally at the same time as it is zooming in.[50] Disney used his system first in the 1937 short, *The Old Mill*, and then in most of the features until *The Jungle Book* (1967), after which it was abandoned in favour of computer technology.

48 Interview with Yuri Norstein, 16 April 2000, Moscow.

49 From an unpublished manuscript by Yuri Norstein distilling his lectures on animation. Translated by Natasha Synessios.

50 More details on the Disney multiplane from the Mouse Pad website: http://www.ggdc.org/mp-100multiplane.htm

Now, in the early 1970s, Norstein and Zhukovsky started developing their own multiplane system. It was very low-tech. Unlike Disney's machine, which needed several people to operate it (apart from anything else, the Disney people would carefully calibrate the distance between the levels in order to emulate classical perspective which, as we shall see below, Norstein considers unnecessary), Norstein's needed, at a pinch, only one, though in practice both animator and cameraman would normally be present, the latter attending to the lighting etc. Norstein and Zhukovsky's prototype, used on *The Heron and the Crane*, consisted of a normal, fixed-position animation camera, looking down on to glass sheets which held the cut-outs – a maximum of three sheets, moveable to any distance from the camera and from each other, with the possibility of more layers if necessary, but any additional levels would not be moveable. Now, if the sheets of glass were raised or lowered between shots, the fixed-position camera could simulate live-action camera moves, with distinct spatial foreshortening. This creative treatment of space chimed perfectly with one other innovation seen in *The Heron and the Crane*, which was also to reverberate all the way up to *Tale of Tales*.

This was the influence of oriental art. Though *The Heron and the Crane* is a Russian folk-tale, and though the setting is semi-classical, with ruined Greek columns, the style is nothing like the Romanticism that might seem to suggest. As we have seen, Norstein had at an early age developed an interest in oriental painting, poetry and philosophy and with this film a definite oriental influence overflowed into his work. And this was not only a matter of inclination: the laws of physics, as embodied in the multiplane animation stand, also had their effect.

Mikhail Iampolski, in a detailed article in *Iskusstvo kino*, dealing specifically with the influence of oriental art on *The Heron and the Crane* and Norstein's next film, *Hedgehog in the Fog*, points out two main differences between oriental and Western art. These are, firstly, that oriental art employs no linear perspective and, secondly, that it embodies a greater measure of 'conditionality', i.e. there is a greater emphasis on change and things are portrayed appearing, disappearing, moving, changing rather than in the static condition of most Western art.

> Thanks to the fact that [Norstein's] image has real spatial depth and does not have to imitate perspective, a new feeling for the world is generated, completely different from that in traditional animated films. […]
>
> However, the organisation of space into tiers creates a world not of real space but of quasi-space. In this world there is no linear perspective, no vanishing point for those imaginary lines converging into the distance, which organise scale and are the axes on which objects are threaded. The world of Norstein's animated films is structured at the same time in three dimensions and in two dimensions. The depth of the image is hypothetical, because it is not continuous, as in classical European painting, but disjointed, discrete. Before us is a hierarchy of tiers, of painted stage sets, 'flats', spaced out from each other, the

distance between which is almost arbitrary. The viewer is not in a position to perceive and evaluate the real distance between the nearest level and the furthest, which is at the same time both infinite and minimal, because the scale of measurement is imaginary. [...] This flat, stage-set structure of space is also fundamental to Chinese and Japanese classical painting. For in oriental painting depth is constructed by the juxtaposition of a foreground and backgrounds which are not related to each other in terms of perspective and are linked only by the capricious interplay of lines and colour.[51]

He points out that classical Chinese landscape consisted of at least two tiers, with part of the landscape – a tree, an architectural feature, people perhaps – on the front tier, with hills, ravines, rocks appearing out of the mist in the background. Norstein's films are, he feels, based on the same image structure, and mist is a similarly important design element in them.

He compares the image structure of *Heron* with this oriental norm, highlighting Norstein's seemingly perverse decision to shoot the birds' rapturous waltz so that they are partially obscured by architectural features in the foreground.

It becomes clear that this film is the most important forerunner of *Tale of Tales*, prefiguring it in so many respects. Firstly, the combination of comedy with melancholy, more often found in live action cinema (for example in the Fellini films Norstein had seen in Moscow in the 1960s), was now seen, unusually, in animation. *Tale of Tales* would run a similar gamut of moods, from the tragic to the wistful to the outright comic. Then there was the importance of the elements – rain, fog and wind – to dictate mood and to act as punctuation in the structuring of the story, a technique that would be deployed to very sophisticated effect in *Tale of Tales*. One

Fig. 30. Beauty in desolation. The Heron and the Crane. *[Courtesy Films By Jove]*

51 'Palitra i obyektiv', *Iskusstvo kino* 2 (1980), p. 97.

Fig. 31. Hedgehog in the Fog. *[Courtesy Films By Jove]*

might also include fireworks in this category. Not natural elements, of course, but they do create mood and provide punctuation. The fireworks motif, occurring in *The Heron and the Crane* as an ironic counterpoint to the birds' inability to reconcile their differences, will be re-used in *Tale of Tales* to poignant effect to suggest WWII Victory celebrations going on in the background while a fallen soldier is commemorated in the foreground. Finally, there is the sense of beauty in desolation, Norstein's penchant for the run-down, the abandoned, the weather-beaten, which could again be linked to oriental influence – the belief that objects are endowed with life and breath, and that death and disintegration are a vital and beautiful part of life. Just as in *Tale of Tales*, a major theme of *The Heron and the Crane* is the ephemeral nature of life and the beauty of objects, homes, ways of life even, on the verge of disintegration.

Norstein's next film, *Hedgehog in the Fog* (*Yezhik v tumane,* 1975) is based on a children's story by Sergei Kozlov. In it a small hedgehog, with a curious nature and a philosophical bent, goes to visit his friend the bear but on the way, lost in the fog, he meets a horse, a dog, an owl and a fish. The multiplane animation stand had been used in the earlier film to limited effect. Here, however, it gives the viewer a new kind of mobility around the set. By now cameraman Alexander Zhukovsky has removed the fixed animation camera and, with the help of an old tripod made in the 20s or 30s, rigged up a movie camera (adapted so as to be able to take single frames) on top of the animation stand. The camera can now move horizontally as well as vertically, and the tripod head can be tilted to vary the camera angle. These adaptations produced fluid camera movements, complex close-ups and pans, creating the kind of space we previously saw only in live action – never before in animation.

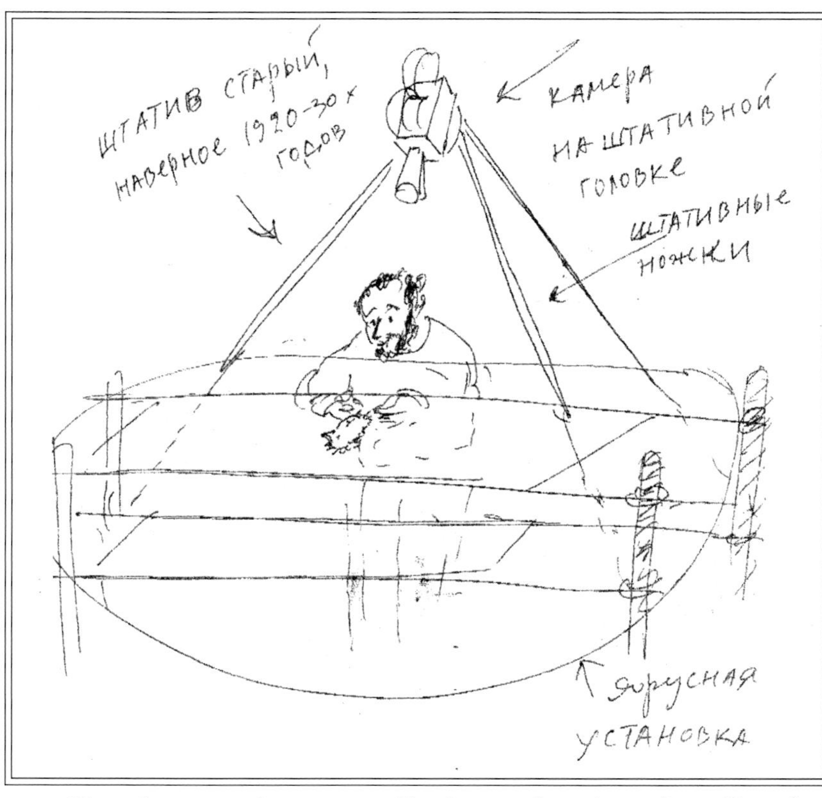

Fig. 32. Norstein's multiplane animation stand, as used on Hedgehog in the Fog. *Drawing by Norstein.*

Here the expressive nature of backgrounds and weather effects first seen in *The Heron and the Crane* reaches a peak. The fog, appearing and disappearing to reveal parts of the hedgehog's world, lives and breathes. It becomes perhaps the most important character in the film. Iampolski again makes the comparison with Chinese artists:

> Water, fire and smoke represent a concentrate of the intangible, the flowing; they are formless fillers of space and are hard to represent in painting. With Norstein literally everything is built on the introduction of these 'primary elements' into the painted fabric of the films.
>
> Likewise, in the stage-set structure of oriental painting mist and water play an enormous role. [...] They are above all expressions of the intangible fluidity of the Tao principle.[52]

One way of achieving these sublime effects of space and weather was prosaic in the extreme – Norstein and Zhukovsky created a diffusion screen by allowing dust to gather on the glass. Sneezing in the studio was forbidden. Norstein tells an anecdote about a talk he gave in Sweden. He was asked how he managed to create such a sense of light and airiness. 'You can't achieve this effect in your country,' he replied, to general consternation, '... because you clean your glass every day.'

Hedgehog in the Fog was, incidentally, a big success in Soviet cinemas, so much so that its title has passed into the language – though not in a very appropriate way for such a lyrical and refined work. For, if someone is

52 Ibid., p. 98.

Fig. 33. Tale of Tales: *boy plus apples.* *[Courtesy Films By Jove]*

drunk, he is said to be walking 'like a hedgehog in the fog'! Norstein seems to take this as a compliment.

But it was not only technical and artistic developments that were taking place during this period. Other things were changing in Norstein's life which were certain to feed into *Tale of Tales.* His two children were born, Borya in 1968 and Katya in 1970. This must have led him into more introspection about his own childhood and that of his generation. Lullabies would certainly have been sung at bedtime and it would be strange if this had not prompted some thought about the eponymous little wolf.

Fatherhood must also have prompted renewed thought concerning the fragility of peace and the problems of determining the right priorities in peace-time, when selfishness takes over in the absence of an obvious common cause. Around this time Soviet society was run by a set of not very inspiring role-models. Norstein himself had suffered from the ideological idiocy of the studio heads over *25th – the First Day* and (probably) from anti-Semitism in the studio and (possibly) from jealousy over the success of *The Fox and the Hare, The Heron and the Crane* and *Hedgehog in the Fog.* These had been shown at festivals all over the world to enormous acclaim and won prizes at Zagreb, Annecy, Tampere, Melbourne, Odense, Chicago, New York and Espinho – but not once had Norstein been allowed to attend an overseas festival. Seeing this kind of pettiness all round him, he must inevitably have feared for the future of such a society – for the future of his children. These fears certainly fed into the winter sequence of *Tale of Tales,* which as well as an idealised view of childhood (a child eating a giant apple and communing with crows) also offers a warning in the person of the drunken, bullying father.

These thoughts might well have led to some reflection about the value

Fig. 34. The drunk and the nag. A warning to parents in Tale of Tales. *[Courtesy Films By Jove]*

of communal life as it had been lived in Maryina Roshcha. In 1967 Norstein and Yarbusova had moved to Belovaya Street, not far from Maryina Roshcha, and in 1970 to Belyayevo, a suburb consisting of typically Soviet concrete blocks (similar to those seen in a brief shot across the valley when the Little Wolf is left alone at the old house). It was the move to Belyayevo, which itself had been built on the remains of a rather more human suburb, not dissimilar to Maryina Roshcha, which prompted thoughts of a film on the subject. For Norstein knew the tenants of Maryina Roshcha would also be given notice sooner or later, and would have to go their separate ways.

> And I imagined that, before that was to happen, we might all have got together, everyone who'd ever lived in that house. It would be a warm autumn day when the sun was still hot. People would carry out tables, and drag out from the corridors their bedside tables, grey, blue, with oil-cloth congealed on to them, marked by knives and hot frying pans, burned by irons... They would set them up in the yard and cover them with one big white tablecloth. And the shades of the dead would appear at the table, on an equal footing with the living. And a conversation would start up. At first nostalgic and then, as it got more lively, louder and louder, gradually tipping over into squabbling... There would be shouts and people calming each other down... And out of the conversations and memories a story would come together, gradually revealing the life of the house.[53]

At this stage, given the still limited range of themes normally dealt with in Soviet animation, Norstein was not envisaging this as an animation project. Seven years later, the news that the whole of Maryina Roshcha was finally to be demolished to make way for even more concrete blocks suddenly made it imperative for Norstein to take the plunge and, by one means or another, capture on film a way of life that was about to disappear.

53 'Metafory', Part 2, *Iskusstvo kino* 8 (1994), p. 92.

Fig. 35. Tables and tablecloth in Francesca Yarbusova's sketch for Tale of Tales.

This period had been eventful on both professional and personal levels, furnishing experiences that would feed directly into *Tale of Tales*. It had been a period of conscious reflection as well as a subconscious processing both of memories and of the literature Norstein had been devouring since his youth. Many of these elements would end up in *Tale of Tales*, and only later would Norstein try to disentangle which bits came from which sources. For the moment they remained a 'mix of micro-histories, molecular episodes, metaphors, which had been living inside me, infusing each other, all the time.'[54]

54 Ibid.

5

The treatment

Soyuzmultfilm 1967 – July 1976

Poetry from garbage …

Norstein's 'mix of micro-histories' stayed inside him for a long time, outliving the urge to compile them into a live-action film. Yet he was still convinced that these diverse bits and pieces could be fitted together somehow: 'If all these elements were living in me at the same time, then that meant something was uniting them. A certain nerve. It just couldn't be otherwise.'[55] Yet no way of doing so sprang to mind. Help was at hand, however. Talented as Norstein was as a generator of ideas, he, like all directors, was not supposed to write the scripts for his films; for Goskino had decreed that scripts had to be written by a certified writer, i.e. a member of the appropriate union. Thus, he turned to his friend, the writer Lyudmila Petrushevskaya.

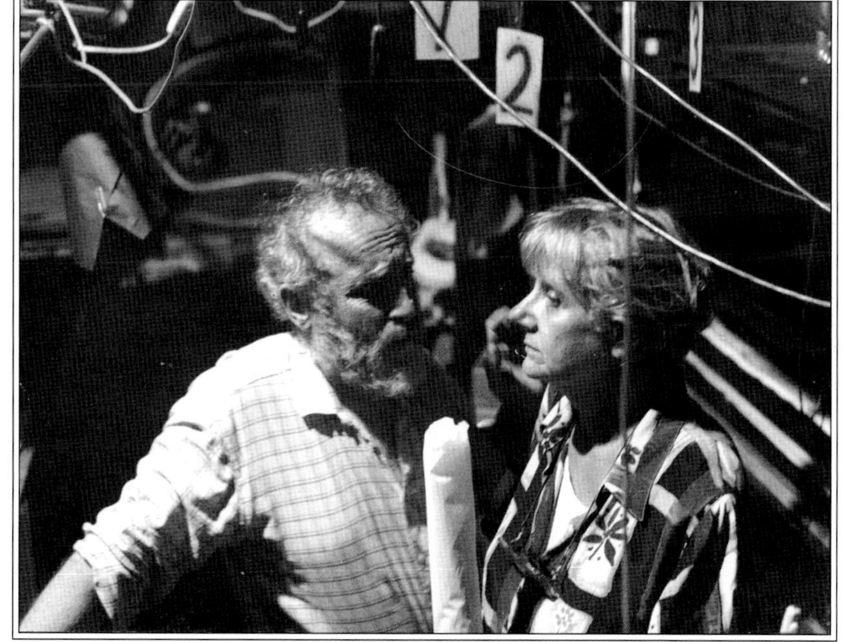

Fig. 36. Norstein with Lyudmila Petrushevskaya. [Photo Tatyana Usvaiskaya]

55 'Dvizheniye … Glavy iz nenapisannoi knigi', Part 1, *Iskusstvo kino* 10 (1988), p. 114.

Jumping forward for a moment, to approximately 1988, and westwards to London, an anecdote from my personal experience may shed light on what an extraordinary decision that would have seemed at the time to any onlooker. In the late 1980s I was still eagerly pursuing my Russian studies and by now also trying to acquaint myself with Russian literature, of which I was pitifully ignorant. In the context of a Russian language course in London, taught entirely by Russians brought over from the USSR, I found myself in a lecture about new trends in Soviet literature, and Petrushevskaya was one of the three writers singled out. We students were asked whether we had heard of Petrushevskaya and knew anything she had written. In the absence of any other raised hands, I tentatively ventured the fact that I knew she had written the script for *Tale of Tales*. The lecturer (an eminent academic from one of Moscow's top literary institutes) tried to be polite, but failed. He told me that she certainly had written no such script and, he snapped, if she ever did write a script for a cartoon it would turn out to be a horror film.

Petrushevskaya is now very well known in Russia, and is one of its most successful writers of short stories and plays, some of which have been translated into English. She came to public attention in the Soviet Union in 1988 when three of her plays, *Three Girls in Blue* (*Tri devushki v golubom*), *Cinzano* and *Columbine's Apartment* (*Kvartira Kolombiny*) – which had previously been performed, but only in the tiniest of venues – were finally allowed for publication. Such celebrity had not always been hers. She began writing, unpublished, at the end of the 1960s. After some limited success in the early 1970s, her work was totally barred from publication from 1974 until 1982. Subsequently, in the years leading up to *glasnost,* it was gradually released, bit by bit.

In the circumstances the ban was not surprising. Her work (now classified by academics as belonging to the 'tough and cruel' school of alternative literature) was thoroughly shocking to a Soviet readership brought up on the bland products of Socialist Realism. Reflecting the depressed state of the country's citizens during the Brezhnev period (the time of 'stagnation'), it was not overtly critical of the system, but social problems such as overcrowding lay not far beneath the surface. Her main theme is the compulsion of family members to manipulate and torment each other. Very few of her characters are likeable, for she quite mercilessly shows the pettiness and underhandedness even of the downtrodden women who tend to be her heroines. The men are almost without exception violent, drunkards and spongers. The suffering on display is indeed shocking, and all the more so because it is overlaid with a black humour and because it has the ring of truth. Petrushevskaya's stock-in-trade is dialogue, and she spends much of her time travelling Moscow's underground simply absorbing the dialogue she hears around her, which she then transfers to the page, non sequiturs and all.[56]

Given that Yuri Norstein was trying to hatch a wistful film about memory and childhood, without dialogue and with a poetic detachment from the details of everyday life, it does indeed seem extraordinary that Petrushevskaya should have been his choice. She herself was surprised.

56 Some of Petrushevskaya's more recent stories have abandoned the kitchen sink in favour of experiments with contemporary fairy-tales.

Apart from anything else, she worried lest her own banned status might rebound on Norstein, who was already not much liked by his bosses.

Norstein, strangely, had at that time not read or seen very much of Petrushevskaya's work, but did not feel that her previous work was that important. More so was the strong relationship he had built up with her since they had first met in 1967 (thanks to Arkadi Tyurin, whose brother worked with Petrushevskaya's husband). Petrushevskaya put it this way:

> You know, people recognise kindred spirits. It's very strange. It happens the world over. Because you know everything can collapse, and usually does. Love, business relationships. Yura [the diminutive form of Yuri] and I have known each other now for 34 years. He became someone I just had to work for.[57]

Much of this mutual respect probably stemmed from their shared background. For, like Norstein, Petrushevskaya came from a family that had suffered under Stalin (in the camps, in her case). Both were children growing up in the euphoria immediately after the war and both realised that the community spirit, evident during war-time and remaining during the post-war period when most people lived in communal flats, had disappeared since that time, leaving a dangerous lacuna.

But this was not the only thing that qualified her for the job. Unknown to the general public (and the academics), Petrushevskaya's literary output was not limited to the 'tough and cruel'. She also wrote children's stories, for her own children, though these were never published. Not only does she like children, but Norstein feels she understands them and even retains some child-like qualities herself. When I asked him what he most liked about Petrushevskaya, it was her truthfulness. 'Like a child, who hides nothing and looks you in the eye and tells the truth without thinking about it, just saying what she thinks.'[58] She also – again quite contrary to her 'tough and cruel' type-casting – loved animation. Or rather she had begun to love animation after seeing what Norstein and Tyurin were doing on *25th – the First Day*: 'Until then I'd always considered animation as something inferior, useful only for practical applications. For children.'[59] Now she was a convert and became, in addition, passionate about the puppets used in model-animation. At one stage she desperately wanted to become a puppet-maker. She told me that she had once applied for a job as cleaner in the studio, simply in order to be near the puppets, but was turned down by the studio head. I think she was exaggerating – but she is a complex and perhaps headstrong woman and anything is possible … Finally, Petrushevskaya's links with animation were cemented when, some time in the early 1970s, Norstein introduced her to script editor Natasha Abramova, and Petrushevskaya joined the latter's group of writing protégés. She did produce some scripts around that time, though nothing came of them.

Throughout this period Petrushevskaya and Norstein remained close friends and they developed two projects together, one based on Dante's *La Vita Nuova* and one about Mayakovsky, key poet of the Revolution, and his love for Lily Brik.[60] These, too, failed to get the go-ahead. During this time Petrushevskaya rejoiced with Norstein in his triumphs with *The Fox and*

57 Interview with Lyudmila Petrushevskaya, 15 April 2000, Moscow.

58 Interview with Yuri Norstein, 15 April 2000, Moscow.

59 Interview with Lyudmila Petrushevskaya, 15 April 2000, Moscow.

60 Lily Brik, her husband Osip Brik (a leading theoretician of revolutionary art) and Mayakovsky lived for some time in a *ménage à trois*.

the Hare, *The Heron and the Crane* and *Hedgehog in the Fog*. However, being a very outspoken person, she was the one to take the bull by the horns and tell him that he had come to a dead end with *Hedgehog*:

> I feared he may be offended, but [...] he wasn't. [...] People were always pulling Yura towards the heights of romanticism and magic. [...] But at that moment another direction came into his mind – poetry from garbage, the poetry of the everyday, the poetry of insignificant things. And my own ideas coincided with his. This is the most powerful material you could find. Anna Akhmatova wrote:
>
> > I don't need martial hosts arrayed in odes
> > And the charm of ornamental elegies.
> > For me, everything in poetry should be out of place,
> > Not what people think it is.
> >
> > If only you knew from what rubbish
> > Poetry grows ...[61]
>
> And this everyday life that Yura was carrying within himself – you couldn't make a beautiful film out of it unless you truly loved this garbage, these insignificant and even ugly things. What can be beautiful in the garbage of an abandoned house? What can be beautiful in the figure of a forgotten old woman? Or that of a drunkard? [...] In the final analysis, love is the most important thing. And Yura loved his childhood and all the people living round his yard, every floorboard and lintel in his flat, the old women poking their stoves ...[62]

Norstein himself recognised how different his 'micro-histories' were from the content of the other animation produced at Soyuzmultfilm: 'I had an idea and some images in my head, but they were very strange. Nothing fitted together and nothing seemed right for animation. Or not for animation as we knew it. [...] The film was a protest against the animation of that time.'[63] So Norstein invited Petrushevskaya to collaborate on the script of his film. She said yes, with pleasure, but she was going into hospital in two days to have a baby, so could it wait for six weeks. Six weeks later, the collaboration began. Of necessity, it took the form of walks in the park, with baby Fedya in his pram.

Norstein feels the fact of Fedya's birth had an effect on Petrushevskaya that made her more interested at that time in the *Tale of Tales* kind of 'garbage' than in her normal 'tough and cruel' take on life: 'Her state of mind, together with my disjointed poetic utterances, had an effect on the writing which was more important than any intellectual thoughts would have been. The film sort of grew out of us ourselves...'[64] They would walk around the park, Norstein telling Petrushevskaya his micro-histories, his childhood memories, the lines of poetry and other quotes which had stuck in his mind, and he would occasionally scribble down an illustration. Petrushevskaya would counter with her own ideas and memories and would season the mix with anecdotes about the people she had been studying in the metro. It was not as idyllic as that might sound. There were,

61 From 'Tainy remesla', written in January 1940. Translated by Judith Hemschemeyer in *The Complete Poems of Anna Akhmatova*, ed. Roberta Reeder, Zephyr Press, Boston/Canongate Press, Edinburgh, 1992.

62 Interview with Lyudmila Petrushevskaya, 15 April 2000, Moscow.

63 Interview with Yuri Norstein, 15 April 2000, Moscow.

64 From *Sotvoreniye filma*, ed. Natalya Venzher, Union of Filmmakers of the USSR, Moscow 1990, p. 47.

it seems, 'a lot of arguments' (Petrushevskaya). Norstein felt that she was 'critical, as a child can be critical'[65] but is satisfied that she unerringly spotted any weaker ideas.

The formula worked, and Petrushevskaya produced, first, a proposal, to put to Goskino for permission to develop the film. The proposal begins:

> This is to be a film about memory.
>
> Do you remember how long the days were when you were a child?
>
> Each day stood alone and we lived for that day – tomorrow would be there for tomorrow's pleasures.
>
> All truths were simple, everything new amazed us, and friendship and comradeship stood above all else.[66]

After this introduction, the meat of the proposed film takes the form of a list – a bit of a tease really, with little clue as to the final shape envisaged:

> The film will feature a poet in the main role, yet the poet does not necessarily have to appear on screen – perhaps his poem could appear [...] A cat is to be seen in the film, a loving creature with a retentive memory. And there will be a single boot, without its pair, found by children in the rubbish. Who could have put it there, a new boot, its sole intact? And that birch tree stump which, as Tvardovsky says, in spring 'will break out in a pink foam', and all the neighbourhood butterflies, beetles and wasps, thin after the winter, will fly to the feast. It will rain, and the rain will feed the earth, fill the boot and the birch stump and wash down the cobbled road. At the end of the street twilight will fall and linger long ...

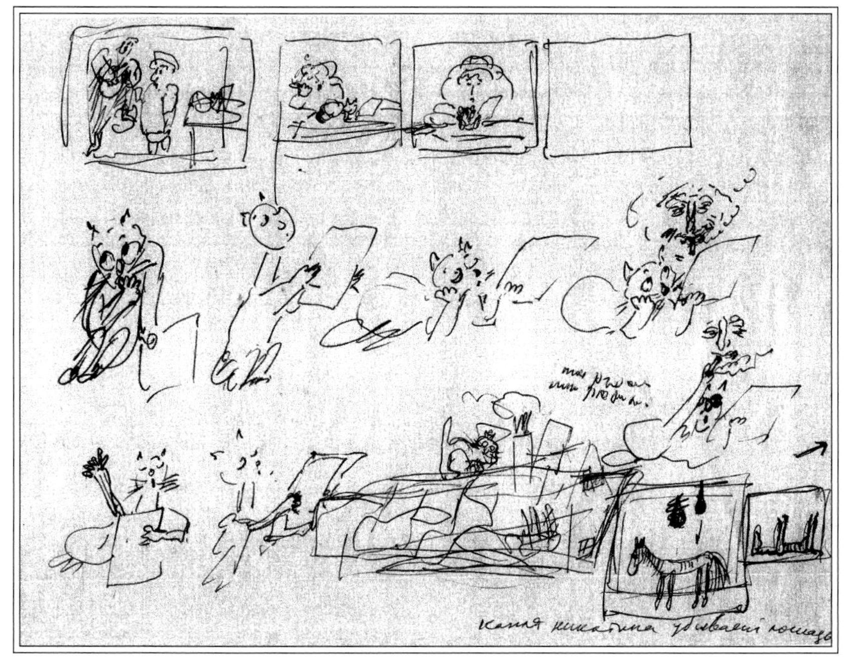

Fig. 37. Some very early story ideas. The cat and the fisherman peruse the poems and a horse appears to succumb to nicotine from the fisherman's cigarette. Norstein.

65 Interview with Yuri Norstein, 15 April 2000, Moscow.

66 See appendix for full text of the proposal.

And so it continues. The title, at this stage only provisional, is *Tale of Tales* (*Skazka skazok*), a title borrowed from a work by the Turkish poet Nazım Hikmet. The poem is a paean to life, corresponding closely to the sentiments that had prompted Norstein to embark on this particular project. Compare the key lines of Hikmet's poem:

> We stand over the water – the sun, the cat, the plane tree and I,
> and our fate.
> The water is cool,
> The plane tree tall,
> I write verses,
> The cat dozes,
> The sun is warm.
> Praise God, we are alive![67]

with the closing words of Norstein's and Petrushevskaya's proposal:

> All this can be organised into a simple but very special story, opening up like a concertina, widening out and then finally squeezing down to one simple sound: 'Life'. For our childhood was at the end of the war, and we must always remember that happiness is each new day of peace. Each new day.

Surprisingly, and perhaps this is a tribute to the simplicity and elegance of Petrushevskaya's prose, this intrinsically very opaque document was given the go-ahead, and on 17 March 1976 Petrushevskaya was commissioned to write a full treatment. This she delivered during the summer of the same year.

The treatment marked the end of Petrushevskaya's official role in the production (though she would constantly return to give feedback and encouragement). Norstein would now produce a shooting script very different from the treatment, and would then shoot a film bearing very little resemblance even to the shooting script, let alone the treatment. Yet Petrushevskaya's contribution had been crucial: crucial in creating a format whereby the micro-histories could be meshed into a coherent whole and crucial in giving Norstein the confidence to work with the 'garbage' of his memories. Also, finally, it was crucial in presenting the material in such a way that the normally suspicious Goskino censors accepted these enigmatic, evocative documents, which bore so little resemblance to anything ever brought to them before purporting to be an animation script.

I'm a poet too ...

It seems there were several versions of the treatment that Norstein and Petrushevskaya delivered in the summer of 1976, though only the final one is still extant. The Russians call the treatment a 'literary script', to distinguish it from the shooting script. It is considered 'literary' simply because it is written out like a story rather than being segmented, with technical notations for the cameraman, etc., as the shooting script is. It is, nonetheless, supposed to consist of a list of the actions to be seen on screen. An early version of the *Tale of Tales* treatment had attempted to do this, but it had got no further than the studio's internal *khudsovet* or artistic council.

67 This translation is my own, from the Russian translation from the Turkish, by Muza Pavlova, in *Nazim Hikmet*, Khudozhestvennaya Literatura, Moscow 1964. The poem has in fact been published in an English translation, by Richard McKane, in *The Penguin Book of Turkish Verse* (ed. Nermin Menemencioğlu with Fahir İz, pub. 1978), under the title, 'A Fable'. I chose to use the Russian rather than the English translation (they are significantly different) because this is the version that Norstein knew and responded to.

The Soyuzmultfilm artistic council was at this time the kernel of what Petrushevskaya was later to call the 'mafia of decent folk'. In the Brezhnev era there was no point in decent people enacting their decency in a straightforward and open manner. They would have been crushed. There was, however, an enormous amount of secret strategy being planned by various upright groups in an attempt to subvert the ideological authorities. The Soyuzmultfilm branch of this mafia would support *Tale of Tales* throughout its pre-production and production and after it was completed, when it was rejected for distribution and shelved for a time. Now, while the treatment was making its way towards the authorities, the mafia ringleader was Arkadi Snesarev. Norstein calls him 'an intelligent, enlightened man'.[68] He was also, miraculously, at that time heading up the studio's script-editing unit, the department Goskino had always relied on so heavily to report anything suspicious but which, at Soyuzmultfilm, especially when Snesarev was running it, it was so signally failing to do. Later, after Snesarev's early death, Fedor Khitruk would take on the mantle of mafia boss.

Thus, an early treatment had attempted a conventional format, with concrete actions listed, and had been a failure. The artistic council had itself taken the responsibility and 'asked [the writers] to adopt this way of writing which we are discussing today, i.e. the recording not of shots, but of a sequence of emotions – those feelings that the authors want to evoke on screen.'[69] Norstein and Petrushevskaya took them at their word.

The treatment falls into four sections. It begins, like the proposal, with the subject of childhood and memory. Unlike the proposal, it is written in the first person, though at this stage the first person appears to indicate an authorial introduction which one assumes will later move, conventionally, into the third person:

> I don't know how it was down your way, but where we lived every evening, every summer evening [...] when the weather was fine they used to play the tune 'Weary Sun' in the park.[70]

It goes on to make the point that childhood will feature in the film, but 'as part of an enormous and magnificent life of the whole world at all times. [...] We want the whole film to say this: People, you are splendid. Childhood is a splendid time.' Then, however, follows a second section, also written in the first person, and couched in far more personal terms. 'And I am a poet', it begins, and proceeds to explain that 'my workplace is the square, the street, the beach. The people. It is they who [...] dictate to me my themes ...'. There follows a rueful passage about the public, who are so important to the poet but whose reactions to his poems are so disheartening:

> I've accepted that – it's fine if my poems disappear into the gaping maw of the crowd.
>
> But – this is strange – they don't disappear. They just lie around under everyone's feet. Someone has torn a little bit off and stuck it on his nose. Someone else is using it to clean out a fish...

68 Interview with Yuri Norstein, 15 April 2000, Moscow.

69 Arkadi Snesarev, minutes of the meeting of the artistic council of Soyuzmultfilm, 28 July 1976 (unpublished).

70 See appendix for full text of the treatment.

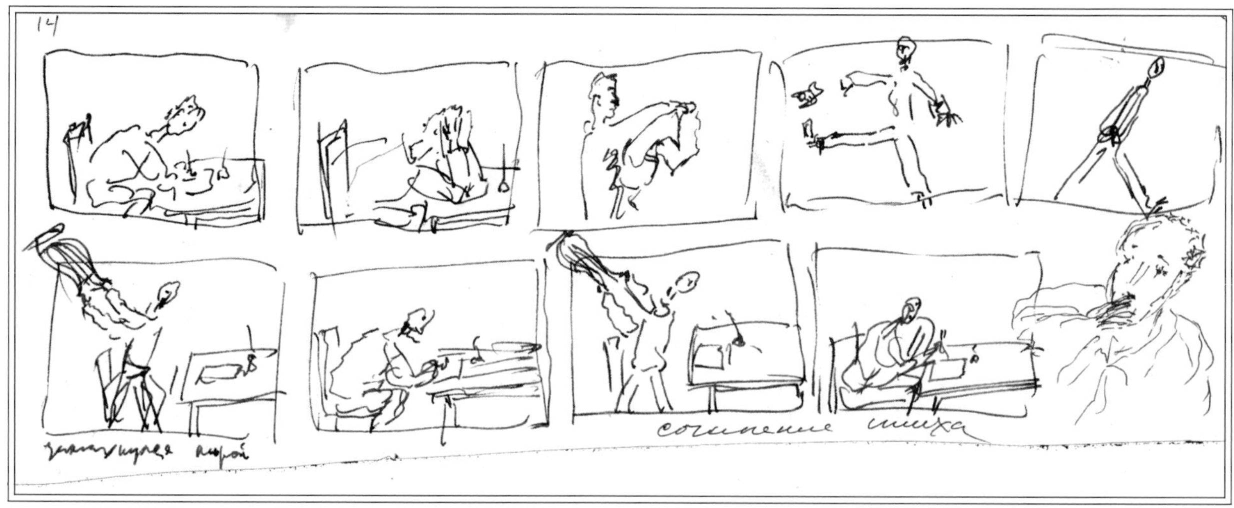

Fig. 38. The poet cannot find an audience. Storyboard section showing his increasing frustration. Norstein.

In a third section, the poet observes a group of characters on a beach – a solitary tourist taking pictures of himself using a delayed shutter release, a man who buries himself in the sand and warns others to keep off, etc – and the poet starts writing poems for them, without their showing much interest. But when another character, a voracious reader, turns up, reads the poems and sprouts wings, he flies over the beach, dropping the poems to their subjects. The poems have a magical effect. The solitary tourist imagines himself getting married, the man in the sand turns into a ferocious bull and another man suddenly acquires the biggest car in the world.

In the fourth section, the poet himself reads one of his poems, and sees houses round a yard, with 'Weary Sun' playing. A woman sings the 'Little Grey Wolf Will Come' lullaby to her baby and this summons the Little Wolf in person, who stares intently at the baby. This is intercut with the beach characters packing up to go home, since it is pouring with rain, while the woman's husband, a fisherman, turns up and invites the poet to supper with the family plus a stranger. While this is happening, the Little Wolf creeps in and steals a sheet of paper from the poet's table – which in due course turns into a baby.

Thus, although Norstein, Petrushevskaya and the Russian critics always talk of the film as dealing with Norstein's childhood, what was actually intended at this stage was a film about the role of the poet in contemporary society, incorporating only a small section dealing with Norstein's beloved house and yard. The poet will be the main character in the shooting script too, and although he is reduced, time-wise, in the final film, he is functionally crucial there as well. So, perhaps the film is not as autobiographical as at first appears? Perhaps the author is simply making a universal and quite abstract point about art and society?

Certainly not. It is very personal. Firstly, Norstein loves poetry, as is all too plain to a translator trying to track down the many and varied quotes which pepper his writings. He also feels that poetry, of all the arts, is the most closely related to animation – to his own animation, at least. He often compares the perfect animation script to a haiku, and has also likened the economy needed in putting together an animation sequence to that required in composing a poem, because both media are so highly condensed.[71]

Furthermore, Norstein not only sees close parallels between the two arts, but surely the same quandary faces the director of a non-narrative, 'poetic' animated film and the poet, penning lofty sentiments couched in not very plain language. Both face an uncomprehending, materialistic public. This is, of course, an eternal problem, and Norstein will quote in his shooting script from Pushkin's poem on the same theme, 'The Poet and the Crowd' ('Poet i tolpa'). Norstein's struggles with his bosses, and his experience of the rough justice meted out to other artists, gave him enough insight into the hearts of men to realise that philistinism is a constant in life. So philistinism is a universal problem – but it is also a problem for Yuri Norstein in Brezhnev's USSR.

Yet, as well as its philistines, Brezhnev's USSR also had a high proportion of citizens whose literary tastes had developed during the relative freedom of the Thaw, and were now hungry for culture of all kinds and would go to considerable lengths to get it. Hence the character of the reader on the beach, and hence the arrival, at this treatment stage, of the Little Wolf. When later asked by Goskino for some clarification on the treatment, Norstein explained that 'The wolf is the main hero of the story. Or rather, he is that dreamed-of viewer (or reader, or listener) imagined by every poet. He, this viewer, will grasp, carry off home and understand everything we want to say.'[72]

Thus, the situation of the film appears to pertain to Moscow in the 1970s. But could the poet represent an animator? It is interesting that the word 'viewer' comes to Norstein's mind in the above quote before 'reader' and 'listener', even though he is ostensibly talking about poetry. I think the poet in the film could definitely be an animator. But could the animator be Norstein? Certainly it could. As already mentioned, use of the first person was exceedingly rare in film treatments. The very fact of its use, and the immediacy of that 'And I am a poet', followed by the delightful detail that prospective readers are in fact using his poems to clean out their fish – all this speaks of personal experience.

Finally, should there remain any doubt as to the autobiographical nature of the 'poet' element of the film, consider Norstein's comments in a Bulgarian television documentary about his career.[73] The film opens with Norstein reviewing his 'workbook', a record of the Soviet citizen's qualifications, jobs, categorisations (Norstein's elevation to 'film director, category 1' is recorded there in 1976). 'Anything not entered in this workbook is held against you,' he says. 'Can a poet's workbook contain thanks for this poem, for that poem?' Then, after a pause – 'I'm a poet, too.' It is therefore, I feel, plain that the 'poet' section of the script in its various versions, and of the final film, is as much steeped in Norstein's experiences and emotions as are the micro-histories of the Maryina Roshcha section.

This, then, is the treatment that was discussed at the *khudsovet* meeting of 28 July 1976. It went down very well. Snesarev and Khitruk were particularly supportive. 'I consider this a subtle and serious work,' said the latter. 'It is magnificently written in this literary form, which itself is a work

71 'Metafory', Part 2, *Iskusstvo kino* 8 (1994), p. 95.

72 'Postscript to the Treatment and Foreword to the Film' – undated, but certainly written shortly after the treatment, during the summer of 1976. Unpublished.

73 *Yuri Norstein*, dir. Vichra Tarabanov, prod. Ecran TV Film Studio, Bulgaria, 1991.

of art capable of standing alone.' Some of the more traditional directors felt this piece of writing did not in fact constitute a script, and envisaged problems with Goskino. (They turned out to be right.) The veteran Milchin was particularly perceptive on the nature of the document:

> Sometimes it happens that a script is written smoothly, as it should be – but the film doesn't work. I think that if Norstein were now to set the whole thing out in words – then there wouldn't be anything left for him to do when making the film. As it is, it is the ground-plan out of which another work of art will be constructed – a cinematographic, plastic, musical work. I have a very deep faith in this director. [...] On a general point, it makes me very happy to know that such works can be conceived in this country.

One of the doubters, Vadim Kurchevsky, not at all understanding what Norstein was trying to achieve, approached him after the meeting to advise him, for his own sake, to abandon this project which he, Kurchevsky, honestly believed was not getting anywhere. He and the other lukewarm *khudsovet* members were however 'decent folk' and fully paid-up members of the mafia. They therefore accepted the majority decision and gave Norstein and the film their full and unstinting support. There was a hitch, and Goskino did not immediately accept the treatment. They simply did not understand it. However, the solidarity of *khudsovet* support meant that Norstein was invited to write his 'Postcript to the Treatment ...' and to attend a meeting at Goskino to explain the treatment to the bigwigs. Finally, and with one proviso – that the shooting script should also be submitted for Goskino's scrutiny – the treatment was accepted. Norstein was authorised to start work on the shooting script that September.

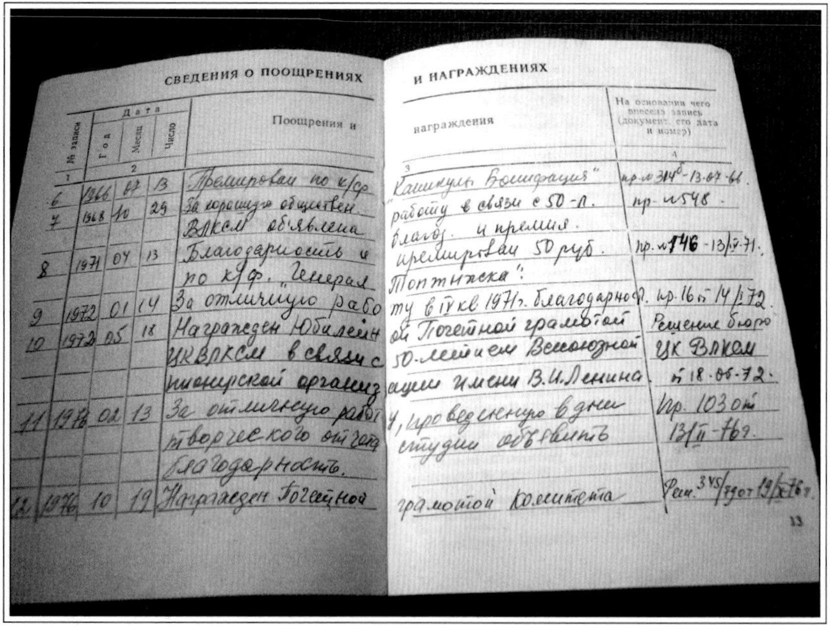

Fig. 39. Norstein's workbook.

6

Pre-production and a false start

Maryina Roshcha/Soyuzmultfilm, autumn 1976 – 1978

Norstein was commissioned to write the shooting script while Yarbusova was to produce design sketches, and together they would then work on the storyboard. (This is the stage where the written script is converted to a series of still images looking a bit like a strip cartoon.) Before starting on the shooting script, however, Norstein wanted to return to Maryina Roshcha. It was about to be demolished, and he urgently needed to photograph what was left of it. Thus, during the Indian summer of 1976, he went off with his close friend and regular cameraman Alexander Zhukovsky, who was also lined up to shoot *Tale of Tales*, to immerse himself in the past.

> The houses looked out at us through blind, unwashed windows. Next to the trees and fences and in the middle of the yards were mountains of things not needed in the new district: old bedside tables, enamel

Fig. 40 (above) and Fig. 41 (left). Maryina Roshcha just before demolition. Two of the houses facing into Norstein's yard.
[Photo Alexander Zhukovsky]

basins, broken tables, shattered plaster sculptures of naiads and remnants of firewood, a rusty cross among them. The skull of someone's once-prized 'M'-type [car] shone white. It was quiet. The yards no longer resounded with children's shouts, or the tinkling of bicycle bells. Maryina Roshcha was moving to a new district ... [...] A woman came out of a door [...] Sasha photographed her [...] – part of the neglected landscape. A bent-wood chair, full of holes, stood on an old nail-box, at the foot of a poplar, with its back to the trunk. I called it 'the poet's chair'. (In the film, the poet sits on such a chair, by the tree.) A scarred burdock leaf hung on the dense wormwood thicket. It had heroically endured attacks from children's bows and arrows and was now slowly dying from its fatal injuries. Sasha photographed it, too. (In the film, a huge leaf, dripping with raindrops, hangs in a damp, autumnal forest.)

The old houses, which had long had their day, held their walls up to the sun, lashed as they were by winds and darkened and decayed from rain. For decades, the houses had been sinking into the earth, their walls caving in, their boards straining. The terrible, irreversible force of the earth's gravity, combining its efforts with those of time, submerged and condensed

Fig. 42 (above left). Maryina Roshcha. The leaf. [Photo Alexander Zhukovsky]

Fig. 43 (below left). Maryina Roshcha. The poet's chair. [Photo Alexander Zhukovsky]

Fig. 44 (below). The poet on his chair. [Courtesy Films By Jove]

the once-noisy life of Maryina Roshcha, turning it into humus. [...] Sasha took over a hundred photographs. The departing world was taking on a fine silver amalgam. When I returned a year later, the bulldozers had taken over, raking up the remains of the past.[74]

It is also recorded that Sasha Zhukovsky struck up a lengthy conversation with one of the Maryina Roshcha cats ...

So some visual motifs in the film – the leaf hanging in the forest, the poet's bent-wood chair, the pile of unwanted furniture – arrived via the most direct possible route from Maryina Roshcha. But not only specific

Fig. 45 (top left). Maryina Roshcha. A cat, almost invisible in the arms of its owner, has just had a conversation with cameraman Zhukovsky. A possible model for Tale of Tales*?*
[Photo Alexander Zhukovsky]

Fig. 46 (bottom). The cat shows the poet how to declaim poetry. Early drawing by Norstein.

Fig. 47 (top right). The cat's demonstration in the actual film.
[Courtesy Films By Jove]

74 Captions for April 2000 *Tale of Tales* exhibition at the Moscow Cinema Museum. Translated by Natasha Synessios.

details were gathered from this disappearing world. For this visit also contributed to Norstein's feeling for beauty in decay, his interest in objects in the midst of change and decline – which also relates back to his interest in oriental art, as seen earlier. A poem that strikes a big chord with Norstein is Pushkin's 'Autumn' ('Osen', 1833), where the poet compares his favourite time of the year, late autumn, to the lingering smile of a girl dying of consumption. Similar emotions must have been aroused by the sight of his old home slowly degenerating and facing imminent demolition.

Having recorded what was left of Maryina Roshcha, he turned his attention to the script and storyboard. It was now that Norstein made what was intended as his definitive decision on the film's title. It was to be *The Little Grey Wolf Will Come* (*Pridet serenki volchok*), which would both reflect the growing role of the Little Wolf character in the film and, as a line from the lullaby familiar to all Russians, would immediately set the scene, preparing audiences to think back to their childhood. At the same time, he set about explaining his design ideas to Yarbusova.

Francesca Yarbusova has acquired a large fan club in the international animation world, and deservedly so. She is arguably the most talented Russian animation designer of her generation. And, given the cut-out technique the couple use, she has a bigger hand in the creation of Norstein's films than art directors would in most other animated films, in that she is involved in a greater proportion of the production. For whereas in traditional drawn animation the designer's main role is to produce the original design ideas (the actual drawings for the film being done by the animators, since the movement is created by re-drawing), Yarbusova not only creates the magnificent design sketches for the films but also the cut-out elements which Norstein, as animator, then moves under the camera. I have heard it suggested that perhaps Yarbusova is being denied her fair share of the credit for *Tale of Tales*. Here I would demur and I am absolutely sure Yarbusova herself would also disagree. Working for any director other than Norstein, she would be able to take the initiative to a far greater extent than she can working with her husband. Perhaps working for other directors she would blossom into the driving force, visually speaking, behind the films she worked on – though the films she has so far worked on with other directors have certainly not been as outstanding as those with Norstein. I suspect the truth of the matter is that, just as Yarbusova's designs bring out the best in her husband's directorial talent, his very demanding, even authoritarian, modus operandi furnishes the parameters Yarbusova needs to produce her own best work. [See colour plates 14–25 for a selection.]

Norstein is happy to confirm that his way of working with his art director is more prescriptive than the approach taken by most other directors:

> When you're making a film, the director must basically make the law. He must be able to see the film in his mind. That's what he's there for. Sometimes designers draw their ideas and directors respond to the designs offered and think 'Yes, that one's right, that one isn't'. But that isn't enough for me. When a director works that way it means he can't visualise the film properly.[75]

75 Interview with Yuri Norstein, 16 April 2000, Krasnaya Pakhra.

Fig. 48. Maryina Roshcha just before demolition. The rubbish will be burned before the tenants finally leave. [Photo Alexander Zhukovsky]

Yarbusova, who does not talk very much, puts it simply: 'Yura's [Yura is the diminutive form of Yuri] an artist, too.'[76] Two art directors on one film (and in one family) could work, if one were a submissive character, but this is not the case here. Edward Nazarov is reputed to have told his students, when trying to analyse this creative partnership: 'Yura is trying to conquer Francesca – but that's like trying to conquer mother nature.'

Yet despite the conflicts and the narrow parameters Norstein sets for his designer, he needs Yarbusova's talent, and he knows it. For one thing, she understands the natural world so well as to have almost uncanny instincts regarding anything to do with nature. Norstein recounts this anecdote about Francesca and a butterfly:

Fig. 49. A pile of furniture in the film waits to be burned. [Courtesy Films By Jove]

76 Interview with Francesca Yarbusova, 16 April 2000, Krasnaya Pakhra.

Fig. 50. Yarbusova working on the Little Wolf.

She gave me a real shock once, when she showed me how a butterfly appears out of its chrysalis. At home we had an enormous bundle of nettles, which was crackling in the jaws of dozens of caterpillars devouring the greenery. Then they crawled all over the room. They attached themselves wherever they could and soon instead of caterpillars there were chrysalises hanging. One beautiful day Francesca said to me: 'A butterfly is going to emerge from that chrysalis now'. I remember we looked and looked and suddenly the flaps of the chrysalis opened and closed. My heart was pounding with excitement. This spectacle was cosmic: I was witnessing the appearance of new life. [...] A pair of wet wings started to push their way through a crack in the outer shell. They were wrinkled, like the body of a baby that has just appeared out of the womb. [...] What happens over two or three years in the life of a human was happening here in an hour and a half. The butterfly was pumping liquid into the nerves of the wings, fortifying the delicate vessels forming the wing-span. The wings spread, became taut like a sail in the wind. [...] They quivered slightly, then started beating, just as an aeroplane tries out its engines and steering mechanisms before rattling out on to the runway. 'The butterfly is preparing itself for flight, drying its wings', Francesca explained. She knew in advance each action of the butterfly, because in her childhood she had nurtured whole bouquets of them. It seems to me that she herself was a butterfly once...[77]

Fig. 51. Title page of the shooting script. The title was The Little Grey Wolf Will Come.

77 From an unpublished manuscript by Yuri Norstein distilling his lectures on animation. Translated by Natasha Synessios.

Fig. 52 The old house, the poplar, the 'golden globes'.
[Courtesy Films By Jove]

Her knowledge of plants, too, is encyclopaedic. He describes their search for the correct plant-life for *Tale of Tales*:

> She chose flowers and wild herbs [...] just as 'In such a night Medea gather'd the enchanted herbs That did renew old Æson.'[78] Bitter wormwood among the rusting iron, small, sweet carnations ... abandoned gardens with the flowers we used to call 'golden globes', now past their prime. There can be no other art director at the Soyuzmultfilm studio who knows nature as well as she does. A shot became infused with aromas, just as a home-made fruit liqueur does.[79]

Since both understand the language of painting, this is used much of the time in their discussions. Norstein will talk of 'texture' and 'scumble' and often quote particular paintings which demonstrate a specific effect he is seeking (unexpectedly, a Paul Klee painting, *Clown*, was used as a model for *Hedgehog in the Fog*.) On this issue they are united and both share similar views on most aspects of art. The problems are mostly related to Norstein's insistence that individual artwork elements should be executed swiftly and not finished off in perfect detail. His ideals in this respect are Picasso and Pushkin – for this great poet, as every Russian knows, peppered his manuscripts with rapid illustrations and cartoons, full of life, movement and humour. As Norstein says of them, 'speed of execution allows a lot of feeling to flow into the line.'[80] Yarbusova can produce rapid, inspired work of the kind Norstein wants and of the kind he feels no other art director could produce. He often recounts the time when he asked her for a wet bush with a baby underneath and received, within ten minutes, exactly what he wanted, with all the spontaneity and life that could possibly exist in a piece of artwork. He feels, however, that she has a tendency to want to continue working on pieces of artwork, which can ruin them:

78 Shakespeare, *The Merchant of Venice*, Act V, scene i.

79 'Metafory', Part 2, *Iskusstvo kino* 8 (1994), p. 94.

80 From an unpublished manuscript by Yuri Norstein distilling his lectures on animation. Translated by Natasha Synessios.

> I'm always telling her not to draw perfectly-finished pictures, as if for an exhibition. We don't need those. What we want is, so to speak, half-finished. What we want is something that will develop further when it's on the screen. If there's no later development the film will be dead! [...] It's a bloody business, a really bloody business. How can you make a designer hold back a little, keep back that bit that will be needed for later development? That's the hardest thing. I know exactly how much needs to be held back. And that's why I'm always drawing, to show Francesca ... [...] If she produces perfectly finished artwork, the result will be no development and it will be dead. And there will be no mystery ...[81]

Obviously, problems in working relationships are magnified many times when the protagonists happen to be married and living together. Petrushevskaya compares Yarbusova to a cow, a sacred cow, the only possible source of the visual magic Norstein wanted for the film and whom he therefore pushed and pulled and squeezed in order to extract the last drop of this vital liquid. Petrushevskaya characterises the production (with, one hopes, some element of exaggeration):

> *Tale of Tales* is the story of the friendship of this whole group of people who were involved, and the people who had the least rights in the matter, who were the unhappiest, were the couple, Yura and Franya [the dimimutive form of Francesca], because each of them was destroying the other. Franya was going to hang herself twice, if I remember correctly, Yura was banging his head against the wall, he was yelling, Franya went on strike. But somebody had to suffer in this golden world. And out of this suffering came the film.[82]

One of the first specific design elements the couple worked on was the Little Wolf. Although he did not appear until a long way into the film (as it stood at that time), he was the character Norstein felt the most happy with and it would be the Wolf's big moment, the last scene, that he would shoot first. As with much in Norstein's films, the basic design and construction is fairly simple – 'you make the texture, you smear it with some water-colour and you scratch over the celluloid and that's all'[83] – but there are always one or two telling final details that provide all the life and character. In the case of the Little Wolf it is the shiny drop on his wet nose, and it is those piteous eyes.

The circumstances in which Norstein found his solution for the Little Wolf's eyes are very typical of his creative method, of this accumulation of detail resulting in Khitruk's 'iceberg'. For almost everything that you see on screen is gleaned from either painstaking research to solve a particular problem, or from one of Norstein's childhood experiences, lodged since then in his memory, or, as in this case, from a completely fortuitous event. It was however a fortuitous event whose importance Norstein grasped immediately. Many another filmmaker might not have done. At a friend's house he happened to notice a rather creased magazine cutting pinned to the wall. It was a picture of a soaking wet kitten with a cobblestone tied to its neck. Someone had just fished it out of the river.

81 From *Sotvoreniye filma*, ed. Natalya Venzher, Union of Filmmakers of the USSR, Moscow 1990, p. 72.

82 Interview with Lyudmila Petrushevskaya, 16 April 2000, Moscow.

83 From an unpublished manuscript by Yuri Norstein distilling his lectures on animation. Translated by Natasha Synessios.

Fig. 53 (above). Plan for cutting out the elements of the Little Wolf. Norstein.

Fig. 54 (left). Norstein's earliest drawing for the Little Grey Wolf.

> It turned out that this friend's son had found [the picture]. But how he found it! He saw a crumpled ball of paper on the ground and out of it, out of this crumpled ball, eyes were looking up at him. Two eyes. And he, being a smart chap, picked up and smoothed out the sheet of paper. [...] The kitten had been, literally a second before, in the other world. He is sitting there, his paws splayed out, one eye burning with a mad, devilish flame, while the other is extinguished. It's already crossed over ... It's quite dead ... How could we fail to be reminded of the eyes of Bulgakov's Woland![84] So we copied the eyes of this kitten for the Little Wolf's eyes. For where the Wolf stands at the door of the house. Where he rocks the cradle and stands with his head on one side ... [...] At these junctures [his eyes] must seem to be looking from the other side of the screen, above all the action. We put them into the most critical and sensitive scenes, where we needed the power of a burning look ...[85]

As for the Wolf's other facial features, Petrushevskaya claims, mischievously perhaps, that Norstein used her profile. But then the Heron and the Hedgehog were also, she says, modelled on her...[86]

While all this is going on, Norstein is also working on the shooting script. This document is written in the traditional form of a script, with precise shot descriptions including running times and footage of each shot.

84 The devil character in *The Master and Margarita*.

85 'Dvizheniye ... Glavy iz nenapisannoi knigi', Part 2, *Iskusstvo kino* 4 (1989), p. 110.

86 *Yuri Norstein, Francesca Yarbusova*, Hôtel de Ville de Paris, Paris 2001, p. 187.

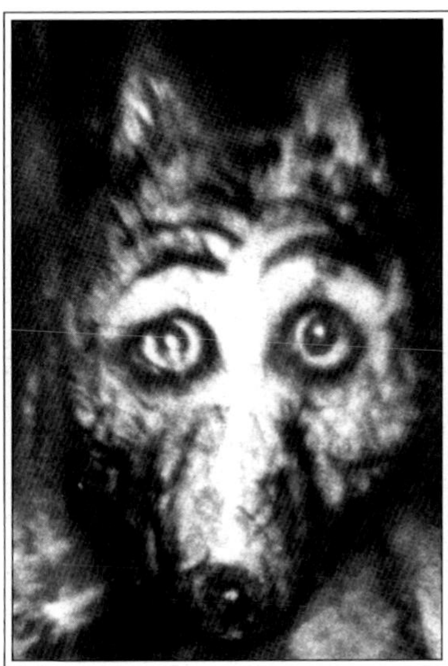

Fig. 55 (left). The Little Wolf. [Courtesy Films By Jove]

Fig. 56 (right). The kitten someone tried to drown.

Being Norstein, however, he could not resist throwing in a couple of quotations, presumably to inspire the cameraman. These are from Pushkin and they describe the problems of a poet when inspiration will not come. The story told is very similar to that in the treatment. It is still the story of a poet, his lack of inspiration and his lack of readers. The old house of the poet's memory still does not appear until the end of the film and the Little Wolf likewise only appears at the end when summoned by the lullaby. This script version is, however, far more defined and it takes a completely linear, traditional, narrative form. There is more detail now – more characters on the beach, for example – and the cat becomes a more important personality, as the poet's companion and critic. The poet is now anchored in the world of the fisherman and his wife from the very beginning, rather than arriving there out of the blue at the end, as had been the case in the treatment.

Thus, it is not too different from the treatment. But it is a million miles away from the final film. So different, in fact, both in terms of content and of structure, that it is tempting to think that this shooting script might have been written to satisfy Goskino, with their predilection for linear stories, while the director actually intended all the time to go his own way and do something completely different. Norstein insists that this is not the case. He acknowledges now that he always had a feeling that this script did not represent exactly what he wanted. It felt stodgy to him – he had hoped for something lighter. But it had been written with the honest intention of filming it exactly as it stood. Apart from anything else, this sense of unease, this feeling that it was not quite right, was at that stage very vague – he had no idea which direction any potential changes should take. So Norstein submitted his shooting script to Goskino, had it approved by them and made up his mind to shoot the film exactly as per the script.

Nowadays Norstein often rails against the tyranny of the script. A filmmaker who prefers the visual guide provided by the storyboard ('you read a storyboard like a musical score, instantly'[87]), he was irritated by Goskino's demand for detailed scripts.

87 'Dvizheniye ... Glavy iz nenapisannoi knigi', Part 1, *Iskusstvo kino* 10 (1988), p. 115.

> [In a script] you lose the most important thing, the immediacy of the poetry, the immediacy of the action. [...] I think a film should be constantly changing, developing. And the only kind of script that can allow for such development is one that is ... like a Japanese haiku. The film grows of itself while it's being shot. And during this time I never look at either the treatment or at the shooting script. Why? Because if I haven't managed to fix anything in my memory, then what's the point of looking at them? To see again that brick that's already been baked once? Those editing plans, written down in words? They don't move! But the storyboard, on the other hand, isn't something you just do at the beginning. You do it every day. It's alive. And sometimes, out of some little detail, out of some action not foreseen in even the most detailed, strict storyboard, sometimes when you're already shooting, a whole scene grows, a whole sequence.[88]

Fig. 57. Andrei Khrzhanovsky's Pushkin Trilogy. *Storyboard sketch for the scene, which Norstein would animate, where Pushkin imagines a conversation with the Tsar.*
[Courtesy Andrei Khrzhanovsky]

While Norstein's attraction to the spontaneous and the 'unfinished' in matters of design is not too hard to achieve in animation, as long as the art director is of the same mind, spontaneity in the scripting process is a far less practical proposition. On the basis of the script, budgets for materials and labour are calculated, so even in the more free-wheeling West such changes are not welcomed. (Norstein and I are both aware that we would not be enjoying the cordial relationship we currently do, had I, when commissioning editor for animation at Channel 4, found myself on the receiving end of these elastic scripts, running times and budget requirements.) In the Soviet Union, with the additional complication of scripts having to be approved by the KGB, any deviation would have been considered seditious as well as un-businesslike.[89]

For these reasons Norstein, despite his misgivings, would set about shooting the film as scripted. But there was a delay of several months before shooting could begin. He was seconded onto a series project (ultimately abandoned, it seems), about revolution, and using works of art from around the world. It was to be called *One Day B.C.E.* (*Za den do nashei ery*); Fedor Khitruk was the director and Igor Skidan-Bosin the cameraman.

When this job was done, still no studio was available for shooting to start on *Tale of Tales*, so both Norstein and Skidan-Bosin moved on to work for Andrei Khrzhanovsky, who was at this time going into production on *I Fly to You in Memory* (*Ya lechu k vam vospominaniyem*). This was the first part of his trilogy of films on Pushkin's life and work, which was to bring to life the poet's doodles in the margins of his manuscripts. Knowing Norstein's fascination with Pushkin, both as poet and artist, he invited his friend to animate a key scene from this first part of the trilogy, 'The Poet and the Tsar' (and would also invite him to animate 'The Poet and the Fashionable Party' later in the series). The first of these, generally rated as one of the highlights of the trilogy, is based on an imaginary conversation between himself and Tsar Alexander I, which Pushkin had written in December 1824. The conversation features a discussion of the poet's work and his attitude to the Tsar, and ends with Pushkin being sent off into Siberian exile. For this scene Norstein was asked to bring to life a self-

88 Ibid.

89 Such unauthorised changes were, however, not as rare as one might assume. As already mentioned, Tarkovsky did it all the time.

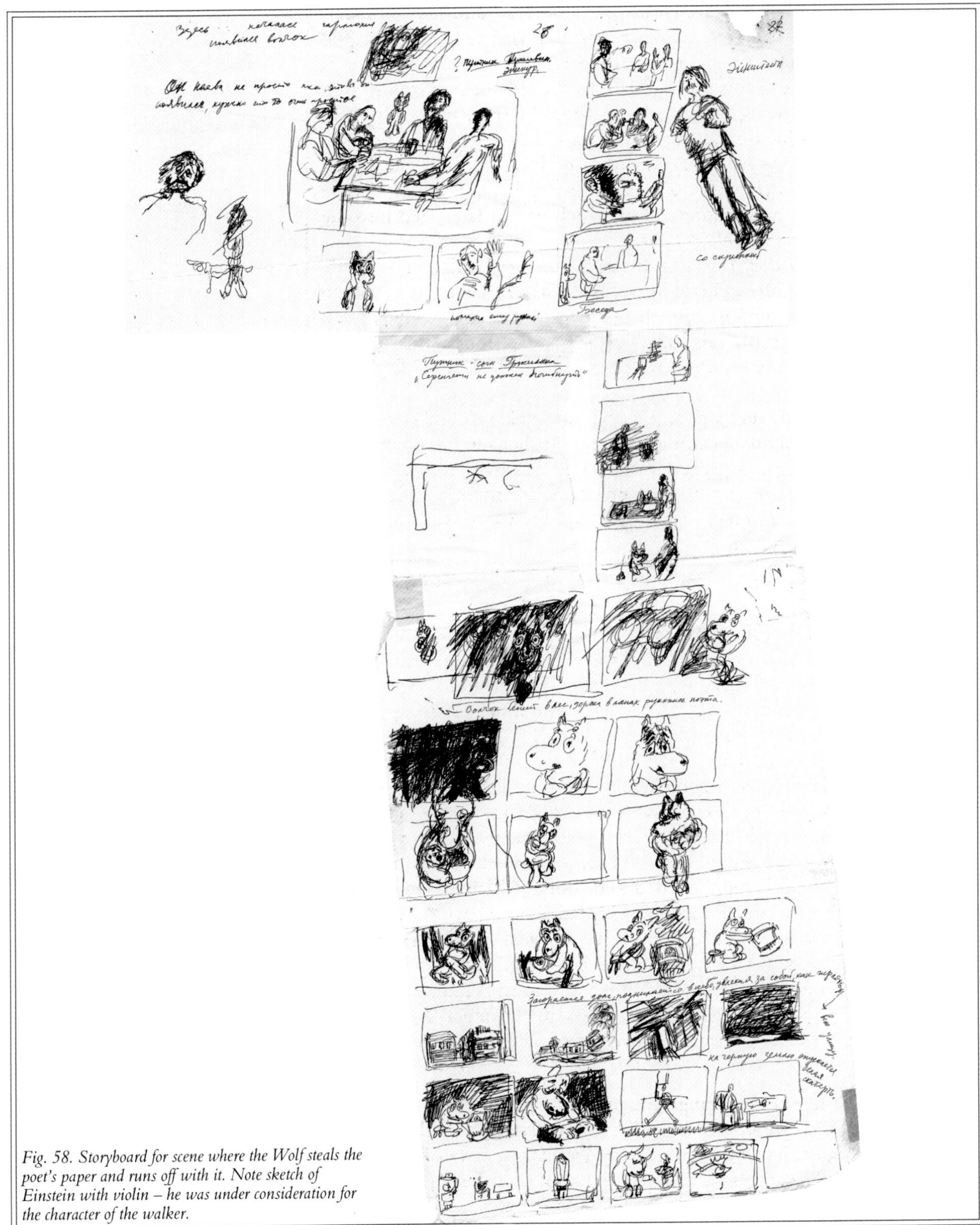

Fig. 58. Storyboard for scene where the Wolf steals the poet's paper and runs off with it. Note sketch of Einstein with violin – he was under consideration for the character of the walker.

portrait which the poet had drawn in the same year, and his animation endowed it with such life and humour that it is hard to believe that the source was one single piece of original artwork.

The significance of this experience was not only further exposure to Pushkin's style of drawing, which encapsulated the spontaneity Norstein so much wanted in his film. It must also have caused him to reflect yet again on the role of the poet vis-à-vis authority. It certainly provided food for thought on the power of the line and the effectiveness of simple line drawings on a white background, all of which would later feed into the poet's luminous world in *Tale of Tales*.

When, finally, *Tale of Tales* was due to go into production, it suddenly became apparent that Norstein no longer had his close friend, cameraman Sasha Zhukovsky, to support him through the film. Zhukovsky had an unfortunate timetable clash. His wife was going into production at the same time as Norstein and his loyalties were divided. He decided to do the job for his wife.

Fortunately, Norstein was able to call on Skidan-Bosin to step into the breach and, after a further trip to Maryina Roshcha to record, literally, its dying moments, the pair started shooting the approved script. But such was Norstein's unhappiness with it that he started with the very last scene of the film, the scene in the forest where the Little Wolf was singing the lullaby and rocking the cradle.

> I absolutely knew that, come what may, this scene would be in the film. But when we were shooting it I kept wondering what we would do when that was finished. I had no idea. [...] I felt that if I didn't know what to shoot next then life wasn't worth living because I was deceiving everyone. When we'd finished that scene, I suggested to Igor, the cameraman, that we needed some time off and applied to the studio head for leave (though I knew this was completely unacceptable during the shooting period). But I had an excuse. It sounds stupid, but there was a good side to working in the Soviet system. There were always problems with the workmanship on the camera or the stand so while they were being fixed that would give you time to think while still getting paid. So I applied for leave on the basis that a lot of this kind of work needed to be done (which was in fact true) and the director, unsuspecting, accepted this. It gave us a month's breathing space. I went to the dacha we were renting at Krasnaya Pakhra – in July, I think, for a month. But I was feeling terrible. I was like a caged animal, yelling at Francesca and the children. I knew I couldn't, physically, stand the pressure much longer. I hadn't told anybody what the problem was, not even Petrushevskaya or Igor – only Francesca.[90]

The stress he was suffering brought him to crisis point one stormy night, when he had a nightmare in which he was flying above the earth and lightning bolts were issuing from his chest, streaking towards the ground and killing people. One uncharitable interpretation offered at home was that this was all the nastiness coming out of him. Be that as it may, the

90 Interview with Yuri Norstein, 15 April 2000, Moscow.

nightmare somehow lanced the boil and cleared his mind. Now he was absolutely sure that the script had to be thrown away and that he must retain only a small portion as the basis of the film. He was now struggling with what was, suddenly, a completely new film.

7

The picture comes together

Krasnaya Pakhra/Soyuzmultfilm July 1978 – July 1979

To reach Krasnaya Pakhra, you leave the metro at Teply Stan and take off to the south-west in an exceedingly crowded bus, its boisterous passengers all laden with bags, boxes and packages. After three-quarters of an hour of bumps, squeals and uproarious laughter, it is Krasnaya Pakhra, and we are pushed and pulled towards the exit by a courteous succession of helping hands. First impressions are not good – the dingy concrete blocks have reached here too. But as we walk further away from the road, we are greeted by far more welcoming, more 'Russian' sights – birch groves, a well, geese and assorted other livestock, meadows, a river and rows of beautiful, traditional wooden houses. There are blue ones, yellow, green, with high gables and elaborately carved, white-painted window frames. This is where the Norsteins have come for many years when they wanted, or needed, to get away from Moscow. Originally they rented but have now built their own little wooden house in the vernacular. Yarbusova now lives there most of the time, with a large,

Fig. 59. Roger Noake and a traditional house at Krasnaya Pakhra. [Photo Clare Kitson]

stately and very clean poodle named Marfa. (Norstein shares his Moscow studio with Pirat, a rather grubby mongrel.)

And here it was that Norstein came after that terrifying nightmare.

> I would try to draw something and ask [Francesca] to draw something, and she couldn't do anything I wanted and I yelled at her – I thought it was all her fault. One day we went out for a walk at the edge of the forest and there in the grass we suddenly found a giant white mushroom [...] and suddenly I felt warm and well. [...] When we got home I was immediately able to rough out a storyboard for a scene that hadn't even been thought of before, a winter scene. I looked at it and said to Francesca 'Wherever did that come from?' It didn't relate to anything in the script. [...] But when I looked at it, it seemed to link in with the war scene and at the end of the scene I saw that fish for some reason. And that's exactly how it was in the film, with the troop-train rushing past, the 'killed in action' notices flying up out of the dark and into the women's hands, and the leaf floating down onto the water. Then silence. I felt such a release. [...] Suddenly these large fragments fell into place and three-quarters of what was written in the script just disappeared.[91]

The winter scene is a mystery to many people. It was especially mysterious at the time to Norstein, who could not at first imagine how such a scene should have popped into his mind. (There is no record as to whether the giant mushroom actually got consumed.) Later he remembered one of those walks with Petrushevskaya where they would exchange anecdotes and ideas. Petrushevskaya recalls her reaction when Norstein invited her to see the scene once it was shot. 'I said, "Where did you get that from?" And he said, "Do you remember, you told me the story ..." "But I told you a completely different story." "Well yes, but ...".'[92] Petrushevskaya's story involved a couple she'd spotted in the metro, both quite hefty, squashed into a seat designed for two much smaller people.

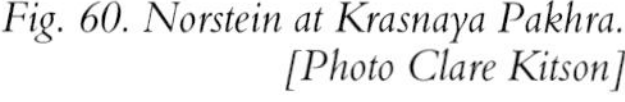

Fig. 60. Norstein at Krasnaya Pakhra. [Photo Clare Kitson]

91 Interview with Yuri Norstein, 15 April 2000, Moscow.

92 Interview with Lyudmila Petrushevskaya, 15 April 2000, Moscow.

Fig. 61 (left). Drawing for the winter scene: nagging mother. Norstein.

Fig. 62 (right). Drawing for the winter scene: drunken father. Norstein.

The woman had been nagging and the man just nodding, resigned. When they had left the train it was the woman who had taken the lead and marched the man off, military-fashion. But in the film the man becomes a drunk and a bully and sports Napoleonic headgear. The woman now has plenty to nag about, and so has little time for the son Norstein has given her. The boy has to look to the crows for company.

> So you see how all this deliquesced into a mythical story. A boy appeared, and the hat, and the park in winter and the apple. It's a short scene, but you can see how brilliant he is at extracting what he needs and discarding what he doesn't.[93]

The apple came into the scene from a totally different source. Norstein remembers that:

> It was one winter, ten years before the film, by the Arbatskaya metro station. I bought the magazine *America*. Snow was falling, as quietly as in that scene. I had an apple in my hand, which is particularly tasty in frosty weather. What bliss – the smell of snow, the smell of the apple, the new issue of the magazine. The magazine fell open at the middle and a picture by Kandinsky poured out of its guts. There was

93 Ibid.

Fig. 63. The winter scene: Napoleon, his wife and child. [Courtesy Films By Jove]

> a happy coincidence of contrasts: the grey-white cold air, the smell of the apple and the painting, which suddenly revealed itself, all created the effect of a sharp zoom in [...] attracting a multiplicity of sensations in a single moment.[94]

This winter episode appeared in the film very suddenly. It was bright, with the kind of saturated colours Norstein normally avoids [see colour plates nos. 7 & 8] and, in the midst of a reverie about the past, it portrayed a contemporary family. And it had not appeared in any version of the script. Yet despite this scene's seeming unrelatedness to the rest of the film, it was for Norstein not only the focus of the whole film but also the catalyst that brought the rest of the film together:

> When this sequence was shot, it became clear where the core of the film was [...] It's important to find a living cell like that. And if it's genuine it begins to accumulate living material around itself without you even doing anything. All you have to do is not get in the way. I didn't know the ending would be like that. [...] The shots sprang to mind spontaneously. I don't know where they came from.[95]

Perhaps the creation of this scene is a milestone on Norstein's 'journey into the light', the voyage into the creative world on which he had set off as a toddler all those years before. Perhaps it was because it had somehow supernaturally imposed itself that Norstein shot the scene in white with bright colours, a colour scheme totally alien to his normal palette – in a subconscious reference to that luminous door at the end of the corridor. Or perhaps, more prosaically, he was feeling a bit guilty about having lied to the studio heads about the reasons for the break in production and about the fact that he was now storyboarding a completely different film from the one they were expecting. Perhaps his enthusiasm over this scene contains just a little element of self-justification.

94 Captions for April 2000 *Tale of Tales* exhibition at the Moscow Cinema Museum. Translated by Natasha Synessios.

95 'Metafory', Part 2, *Iskusstvo kino* 8 (1994), p. 93.

Fig. 64. Edward Nazarov's interpretation of Tale of Tales.
[Courtesy Edward Nazarov]

Fig. 65 (below). Crows in tree -winter scene from Tale of Tales.
[Courtesy Films By Jove]

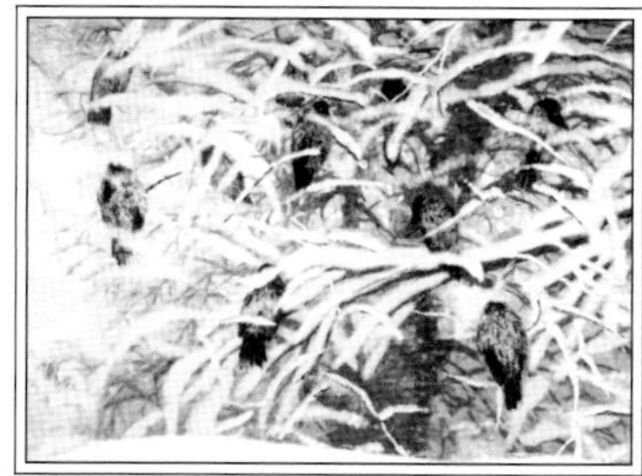

Nevertheless, like the old house sequences, it does have strongly autobiographical elements and it is perhaps not as alien as it seems at first. As a child Norstein loved climbing trees. He and the other kids 'lived in' the poplars in their yard at Maryina Roshcha. He has always loved crows and would watch them for hours as a child, hearing in their spasmodic cawing the rhythms of housewives joshing each other in the *kommunalka*. He was also fond of a particular kind of soft, fluffy snow, and the conjunction of these predilections resulted in a study of crows on a snow-covered tree – painted at around the time he graduated from the animation course [see colour plate no. 6]. Almost the same image was reproduced in *The Fox and the Hare* [see colour plate no. 15] and now here it was in *Tale of Tales*.

Norstein's own children were 10 and 8 years old at the time he was working on this scene, and must have provided plenty of opportunities for observation for this portrait of childhood and of childhood's fertile imagination. But they did not only provide models. They must also have focused their father's fears about the fragility of peace and the problems of life in the Soviet Union of the late 1970s, or in any society where there are no obvious communal priorities to pursue. Remembering the tribulations of his own childhood thanks to officially-sanctioned anti-Semitism under Stalin, he must have been more than a little anxious about his offspring growing up in the pernicious atmosphere of the Brezhnev regime. Norstein's concern is expressed in one of his preliminary drawings for this

Fig. 66. Norstein's drawing of boy and apple for the winter scene.

Fig. 67 (below left). Norstein's drawing for the drunk with the Napoleonic headgear: 'Our contemporary'.

Fig. 68 (below right). Norstein's drawing for the boy in the winter scene: in danger of inheriting his father's hat.

scene. Below the drunk – and the hat – he has written 'Napoleon – our contemporary'.

This scene constitutes an effective warning against the temptations of selfishness and bullying. He chose not to make it aggressive, nor very satirical, but rather melancholic – disillusioned, perhaps. Nevertheless it makes its point – and it puts a child centre stage. For, he says, children learn from their elders and, in accordance with his favourite Tolstoy dictum, the younger they are the better they learn. Thus children are threatened by the aggression of

adults but they are also in danger of taking aggression for the norm and themselves continuing to propagate this norm.

Norstein quickly storyboarded this scene and Yarbusova set to work on the artwork. He then moved on immediately to the war scenes and was able to storyboard all of those too. This link in Norstein's mind between the winter scene featuring a vulnerable child and the war scenes seems to be further evidence that it was this aspect, that of the fragility of peace, which was uppermost in his mind when creating the winter scene.

Then it was time to design the war-time scenes, but little research was necessary, since two of Norstein's 'micro-histories', the memories he had been carrying around for so long, helped a lot. Firstly, the quality of the post-war street-lighting, and then the fundamental design for the figures in the dance scene came to him out of his memory store.

> It seems to me for some reason that in the sixties there was more light, more sunlight. But after the war we lived in twilight. We had wooden lamp-posts with damp patches, and the lamps shone weakly, so weakly that you could even look at the filament ...[96]

He remembered, specifically, an evening when he was returning to the dacha they were renting, passing near one of these puny street-lamps just as a woman appeared for an instant in the circle of light only to disappear again instantly into the darkness. That motif also made its way into the film.

The figures of the dancers came from Norstein's memories of a shooting gallery that he often visited in the park near his home:

> I imagined that [...] the people were sacrificial victims, bound for the slaughter. So we had to draw them like those figures in the shooting gallery, worn, jagged, pockmarked by bullets, somersaulting effortlessly and falling as if dead.[97]

Having storyboarded these two key scenes and agreed with Yarbusova their basic design strategies, Norstein left the production of artwork to his wife, while he hurried back to Moscow to resume shooting with Skidan-Bosin. They shot the winter scene easily and very fast – in only three weeks. Petrushevskaya, incidentally, had been told nothing of what had been going on. Norstein was nervous of showing her the winter scene, partly because it bore no relationship to the script they had written together, but partly also because she is not keen on prettiness. Norstein feared this winter scene might be too pretty for her to take, with its snowy white background and its bright, saturated colours. He need not have worried. She, though initially as puzzled as he was as to where it had come from, loved the scene.

By now the die is cast. The film no longer has a linear narrative and it no longer spells out in detail the story of a poet and his relationship with his public. Now the film is about memory and, as critic Mikhail Iampolski points out, it is also constructed like a memory.

> Norstein's film [absorbs] within itself the tender and the tragic, poetry and grief, interlacing our past with the present in a fantastic synchronisation. This is a film about the memory of a generation whose childhood coincided with the war and whose present consciousness

96 Ibid., p. 94.

97 Ibid., p. 94.

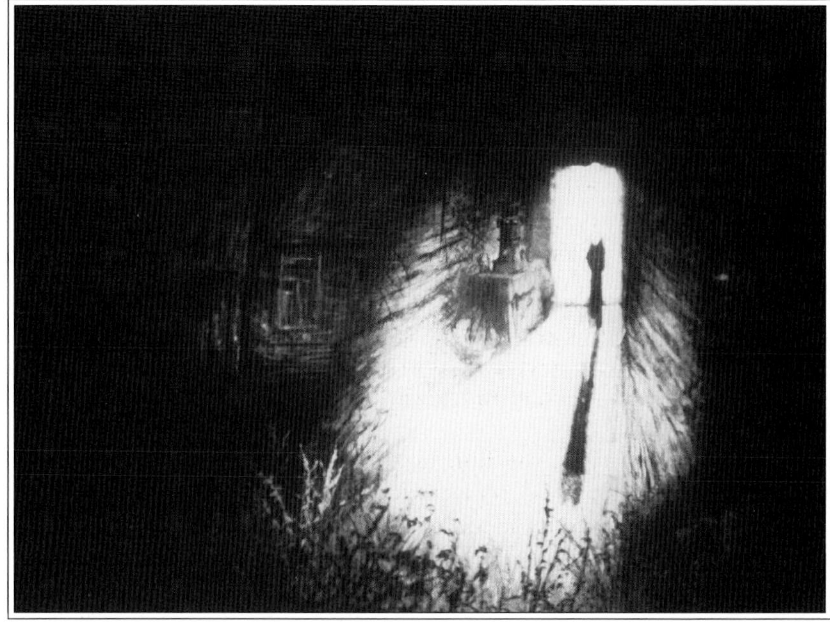

Fig. 69. The Little Wolf disappears into the light. [Courtesy Films By Jove]

is marked by all the polyphonic quality of history. Its originality lies in the fact that all these great and important concepts are embodied in the actual figurative structure of the film. What confronts us is not simply a film about memory, but a film built like memory itself, which imitates in its spatial composition the structural texture of our consciousness.[98]

This is achieved by the construction of a set of parallel worlds: the

Fig. 70. An apple moves from the winter scene into a rainy forest. [Courtesy Films By Jove]

98 'The Space of the Animated Film: Khrzhanovsky's "I Am with You Again" and Norstein's "The Tale of Tales" '. Mikhail Yampolsky, trans. Andrew Braddel, *Afterimage* 13, Autumn 1987, p. 104. Originally appeared in *Iskusstvo kino* 3 (1982), p 92. NB The *Afterimage* article appeared before the author left Russia. He is now established in the United States and spells his name Iampolski rather than Yampolsky.

old house with, nearby, an old street light and the setting for the war-time scenes; the poet's world, where a fisherman's family also lives and a bull and a walker come to visit; the snowbound winter world of the boy and the crows; and the forest next to a highway, where the Little Wolf makes his home under the brittle willow bush. It is as if, says Iampolski:

> ... there exists between these a kind of membrane, easily permeable only by the little wolf scurrying between the worlds, and by several 'accidental' objects, which are the agents of chance crossing from one world into the other.[99]

Apples and giant leaves, as well as the Little Wolf, turn up in different worlds, like triggers conveying us from one memory to another. Babies and breasts also appear in indeterminate backgrounds that seem to sit between worlds.

Unlike the scripts, the film now features the house of Norstein's childhood as the main world, replete with his remembered plants, furniture, neighbours, corridor, light, tango, lullaby and Little Wolf.

The Wolf had previously, in the scripts, been a character in the poet's world and had only arrived towards the end of the story when summoned by the singing of the lullaby. Now, since the re-structuring, the Wolf has become the main character. He still functions as the poet's audience, inspiration and alter ego. But thanks to the parallel worlds and his unique ability to pass between them he can now also take his rightful place in the most natural setting for him: in the old house where the infant Norstein would imagine him nightly when the lullaby was sung to him. The Wolf can become the embodiment of the poet's childhood memories.

> It always seems to me that [the Little Wolf] stayed behind living in the house that I had to leave. And I don't even know what happened to him when they demolished the house. For every house has, and must have, its own spirit. Must have its genius. [...] Why is it that when you enter a particular house or approach some people you feel there's a spirit here, that this house is permeated, saturated with the feelings of the people living in it?[100]

Not only is the Wolf remembered as sharing the *kommunalka* when Norstein was living there: he has remained there after everyone has moved out, as its spirit, the *domovoi* of Slavic mythology, the guardian and embodiment of a home, its inhabitants and all its memories.

Now the rest of the film too was coming together and Norstein and Yarbusova were preparing artwork for the poet's world. This world was to have a very special atmosphere. It was, after all, the world Norstein had imagined at the end of the corridor as a child, where 'eternal happiness, light, a talking cat and bread sprinkled with sugar' awaited him, and where memories remain eternal. Viewers often wonder whether it has a religious significance. I have, in fact, heard both the cameraman, Igor Skidan-Bosin, and Norstein himself refer to it as the 'biblical' scene. Norstein's intention was certainly not religious in the conventional sense – he subscribes to no religion; though he sometimes talks about metaphysical forces present in

Fig. 71. Katya as a toddler. 'A baby's little heel has more religious significance ...' A factor in the look and atmosphere of the 'Eternity' sequence. [Photo Norstein]

99 Ibid., p. 106.

100 'Dvizheniye ... Glavy iz nenapisannoi knigi', Part1, *Iskusstvo kino* 10 (1988), p. 112.

Fig. 72. Dinner-time in 'Eternity'. [Courtesy Films By Jove]

the everyday. 'To me a baby's little heel has more religious meaning in it than the most magnificent liturgy.'[101]

It is this kind of feeling for the mystery and the uniqueness of human life, and for the wonder of natural and warm human relations, that pervades the poet's world. (Norstein, incidentally, usually refers to the long scene in this world as the 'Eternity' sequence). As his inspiration for this ideal world, he quotes a wide range of writers whose works had seemed to incorporate some element of what he wanted to express. These range from a Czech novelist named Ludvík Aškenazy to the Roman philosopher emperor Marcus Aurelius, Walt Whitman's *Leaves of Grass* and Thoreau's *Life in the Woods*:

> When we were working on the luminous final sequence of *Tale*, I couldn't help thinking of what I'd read. It was an interlacing and intertwining, as in a plait, of these impressions. Various visual impressions were also mixed in – drawings by Picasso and Pushkin that had remained in my memory ... and the light that seemed to stream from Pushkin's manuscripts which I'd once seen.[102]

Norstein had indeed been greatly affected by his stint just previously on Andrei Khrzhanovsky's Pushkin film, which had reinforced his feelings for the strength and the emotion that can be conveyed in simple line-drawings. He therefore decided that this segment should be done in an equally simple-looking style [see colour plate no. 12, Norstein's sketches for the scene]. Much of the atmosphere of this calm, quiet, idealised world originated at Krasnaya Pakhra. The fact that it was all designed in long-shot certainly related to his observations there – possibly heightened by the fact that he was a visitor and an urban visitor at that. He was someone who would necessarily be observing from a distance:

101 Fax from Yuri Norstein to the author, 20 March 2001.

102 'Metafory', Part 2, *Iskusstvo kino* 8 (1994), p. 97.

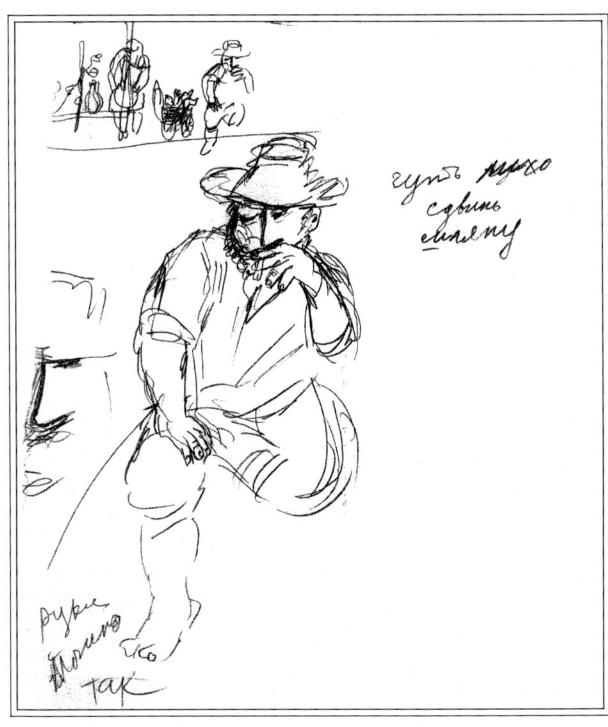

Fig. 73 (above left). At one stage, life in the poet's world was a lot more raucous. A very early design for the fisherman. Norstein.

Fig. 74 (above right). Another idea for the fisherman – a more rakish look, based on a fisherman Norstein had once seen.

Fig. 75. A later drawing for the fisherman, closer to the final design. Norstein.

Fig. 76 (above). At one time Einstein was considered as the model for the walker.

Fig. 77 (right). A preliminary drawing for the walker. Norstein.

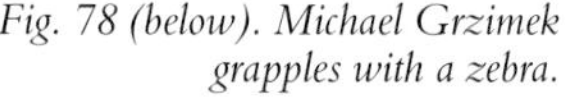

Fig. 78 (below). Michael Grzimek grapples with a zebra.

It was important to communicate the music of the gestures, the pauses, the silence ... I remembered our landlady at the dacha, Fenya, and our neighbour, Nyura. I remembered the tinkling of the cups, their muffled evening conversations, when words are indistinguishable, when the sounds of speech flow into a single stream of utterances, like the murmur of water on the river shallows in the cool dusk. [...] These good women are no longer alive but I think that the thin partition fence at the dacha continues to catch their voices like the sounding board of the cello.[103]

Another vivid memory from Krasnaya Pakhra was the image of farm workers at the end of a long day's harvesting, seen in the distance, almost in silhouette against the settling dust and red sunset, smoking and conversing intently, but not a word audible from where he stood. He would film the 'Eternity' scene in the same way, almost in silhouette, with the figures losing their substance, 'so that the image might be experienced first as an emotion ...' [104]

103 Captions for April 2000 *Tale of Tales* exhibition at the Moscow Cinema Museum. Translated by Natasha Synessios.

104 From an unpublished manuscript by Yuri Norstein distilling his lectures on animation. Translated by Natasha Synessios.

Fig. 79 (left). Early roles for the bull: as dancer and cellist. Norstein.

Fig. 80 (right). At one stage he had to help with the washing. Norstein.

Having established the general principles of atmosphere and design for this key sequence, Norstein and Yarbusova turned their minds to the characters populating the scene. They are humans, not cartoon characters, and Norstein was determined to make them real. He therefore embarked on extensive research for all of them – even those only seen in long-shot with faces obscured, such as the walker. Having scoured various sources

Fig. 81. In the film he skips. [Courtesy Films By Jove]

for a suitable prototype, Norstein finally discovered a book about the Serengeti, by one Professor Bernhard Grzimek and his son Michael. Michael had been killed at the age of 24 in a plane crash, while listing the fauna of the Ngorongoro crater.

> I liked the photographs of Michael immensely. While I was reading the book about him, this man became very dear and very close to me – as though we spent our evenings together at the same table, talking ... [...]
>
> Why do I need all this? When all is said and done, a traveller walks along, in long shot, no one sees him, no one knows who he is. But I need to know who it is walking down that road, because then my attitude to this character and the way I animate him will be completely different. We tried so many different versions back then! There was a slightly tipsy man in a jacket, there was Plato, even Einstein with his violin and his fountain-pen tucked down the neck of his sweater ...[105]

Similarly, a great deal of research went into the 'casting' of the poet himself, even though his face is rarely seen. Again, detailed work, 'underwater' and invisible to the naked eye, contributes massively to the characterisation of the animated figures and the overall humanity of the completed film. Photos of Pablo Neruda were studied, Lorca, Mandelstam and Mayakovsky, but none of them seemed right, and the poet's face was finally an amalgam of them all. Only many years later did Norstein first see a photo of Gumilev,[106] and was struck by an uncanny resemblance to his own, synthesised poet: 'The same profile, heavy eyelids and expressive mouth.'[107] Norstein concluded that perhaps all poets shared one facial feature in common: 'These photos gave the impression of sounds dying away on the poets' lips. As if they were trying out a word in the air.'[108]

The bull, intriguingly, remained in this scene, a remnant from the scripts. (It had indeed featured in Norstein's earliest preliminary sketches, before actual scripts were even discussed.) This character arouses much learned discussion among viewers of the film as to his metaphorical significance. He is often referred to as a 'minotaur', sometimes seen as a reference to Picasso's *Guernica*. Norstein denies any metaphorical significance to the bull, though this is somewhat disingenuous. In the shooting script a very bad-tempered and anti-social man on the beach had turned into a bull in the presence of poetry. This is certainly metaphor of a kind. At first a very bad-tempered bull, he finally becomes a very placid bull who, thanks to the power of poetry, has a vision of a stunning cow standing Botticelli-like on a shell floating by, chewing the cud. It is this poetic bull which remains in the final film to turn the skipping rope for the fisherman's daughter.

Once more, having settled the design ideas with Yarbusova, Norstein returned to Moscow to continue shooting with Skidan-Bosin. Skidan-Bosin is a highly-skilled technician and, like Norstein, very inventive. They are of a similar age and thus share the experience of a post-war childhood. They worked well together on *Tale of Tales*, though the relationship was to sour when they worked together on a later project. Skidan-Bosin's talents

105 Ibid.

106 Nikolai Gumilev, a successful poet in the 1910s, leader of the Acmeist group and husband of Anna Akhmatova. Executed in 1921 on trumped-up conspiracy charges.

107 'Metafory', Part 2, *Iskusstvo kino* 8 (1994), p. 97.

108 Ibid.

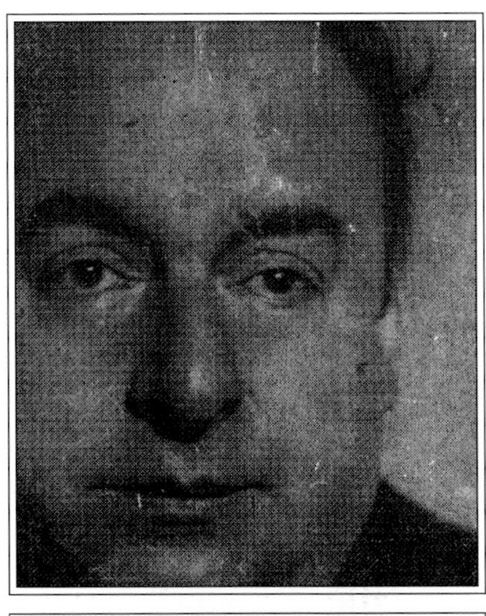

Fig. 82 (top left). Pablo Neruda.
Fig. 83 (top right). Osip Mandelstam.
Fig. 84 (middle left). Sappho.
Fig. 85 (middle right). Anna Akhmatova.

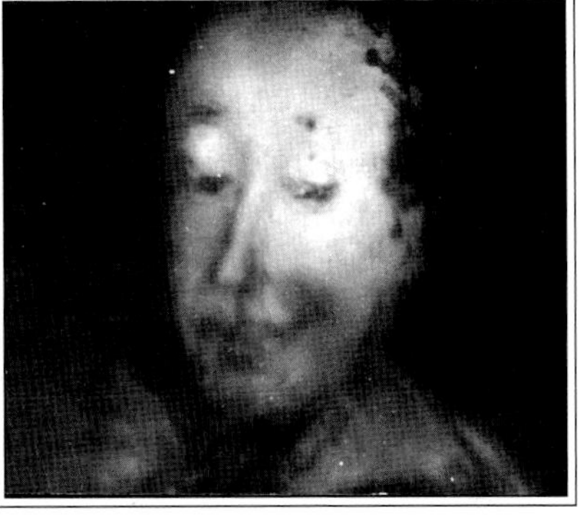

Fig. 86 (bottom, left). Nikolai Gumilev.

Fig. 87 (bottom, right). The 'synthesised' poet turned out to bear a remarkable resemblance to Nikolai Gumilev. [Courtesy Films By Jove]

Figs. 88. Stages in the development of the poet. Norstein.

were summed up in a reference which Norstein sent to the Goskino Pay-Scales Committee in an attempt to get the cameraman to a higher point on the salary scale:

> I.Y. Skidan-Bosin's work on the film *Tale of Tales* can in many ways be considered an encyclopaedia of the animation cameraman's art.
>
> The film was complex in its genre structure and involved such a diversity of artistic problems that one can only wonder at the inventiveness and resourcefulness shown in the camera work. This was achieved, moreover, with no fuss and an absolute readiness for sudden challenges of any kind. Think of the inventiveness of the film: the soft classicism of the first few shots, the baby suckling at a breast, the apple in the forest under the rain; the luminous sequences of the Eternity scene; the sharp dissonance of the war scene; the harpsichord purity of the snow-covered trees; the warmth of the autumn courtyard and the old house; the glass of vodka in memory of a fallen soldier, illuminated by the flickering light of a victory salute; the many complex combined shots involving a variety of different ways of lighting the scene.
>
> Another cameraman might not meet such diversity in the whole of his creative life.[109]

109 Reference for Skidan-Bosin, undated but definitely sent post-1984, since the Los Angeles Olympiad of Animation poll is mentioned later in the document. Unpublished.

Skidan-Bosin, incidentally, did not get the requested rise up the pay-scale because, like Norstein, he was not a university graduate.

Some of the most innovative tricks they thought up together were the sections where live action was incorporated into the animation. One of their more terrifying exploits was the generation of the live action fire when the old furniture spontaneously combusts in front of the old house. They achieved this effect, they tell me, and who am I to question, by hanging a sheet of kerosene-soaked paper on the coat hooks along the corridor in the studio, and then setting it alight and filming it. When incorporating this into the animation a projector and a screen were set up next to the animation stand and a semi-transparent mirror was used to deflect the image of the fire on to the drawn pile of furniture. A similar technique was used for the live action flame on the animated candle in the jar, which is extinguished by the poet's cat, and also for the traffic headlights on the highway and the bowl of hot charcoal on which the Little Wolf roasts his potatoes.

One shot of which Skidan-Bosin is particularly proud is that of the glass of vodka, seen against the soundtrack of a victory salvo celebrating the end of the war. In Russia, when someone dies, traditionally a glass of vodka is put on the table and left there for forty days. At the end of the forty days, it is assumed that the person's soul has departed for the other world, and the glass is cleared away. It seems that by the fortieth day the glass has usually emptied itself.

> Francesca had done a sketch for this but Yura couldn't think how to do it so that it would look good. The shot had an allocation of only 40 frames, a metre [about two seconds]. We both sat and thought and then it came to me that we could put a real glass on the spot, and cover it over so that it wasn't visible. The first exposure would just shoot

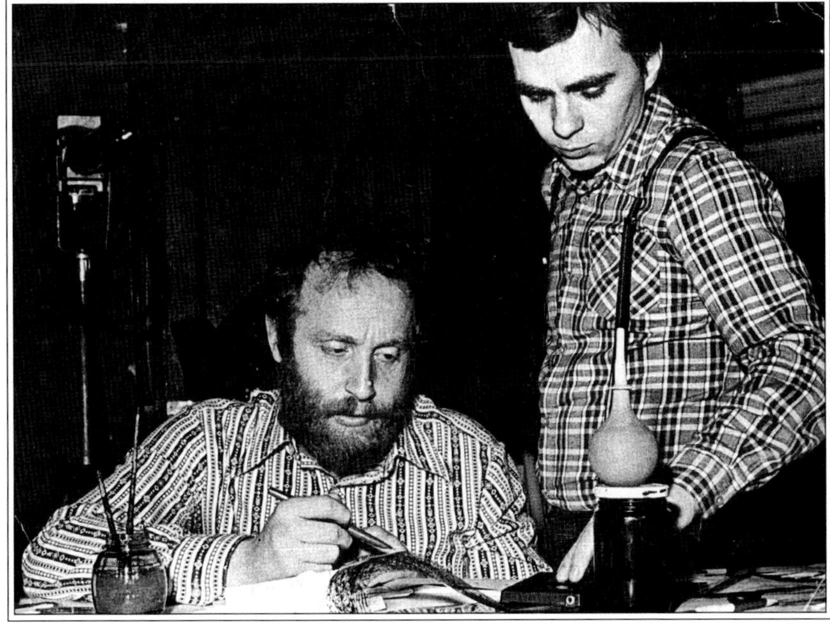

Fig. 89. Norstein and Skidan-Bosin working on Tale of Tales. *[Photo Yelena Darikovich]*

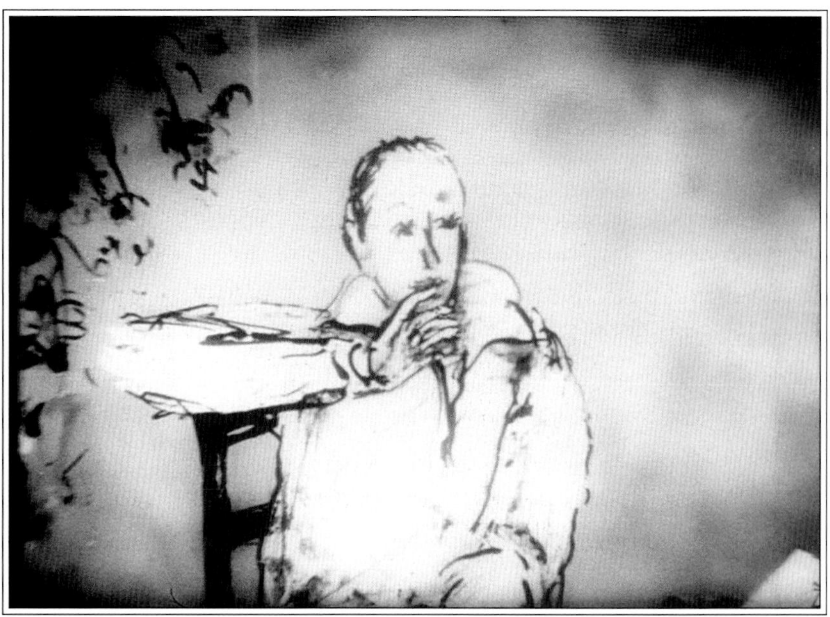

Fig. 90. Shooting on high-contrast black and white stock gave an impression of drawn animation. [Courtesy Films By Jove]

> the background. Then we lit the glass of water and started to move it round. Then the rays of light started to light up the tablecloth as though as a result of the victory salute. When we started doing it we realised that the possibilities were even greater. We wanted light playing around the rim of the glass, [...] then playing on the surface of the liquid, then somewhere on the sides of the glass, then with a separate exposure, on the leaves. So that drops would be running down the leaves, looking like tears. For that shot and those 40 frames we ended up shooting 12 exposures. And when we put them together they didn't look bad. I don't think a viewer would realise.[110]

The 'Eternity' sequence also took a great deal of ingenuity as well as instinct on the part of Norstein and his cameraman. Skidan-Bosin revealed that the secret of its luminous, 'biblical' look was shooting it on high-contrast black and white stock instead of colour stock like the rest of the film and subsequently transferring it to colour film. Apart from the supernatural atmosphere thus invoked, this method also had the more prosaic advantage of concealing the joints of the figures and the edge of the cut-out cel, so that the impression was of drawn animation.

Norstein would later say that Skidan-Bosin had overdone the bleached-out effect, and it is true that it is quite hard to distinguish the image when viewing the film on video. But that probably says as much about the poor quality of the videos and some of the materials from which videos were struck as it does about the camera work.

It is not only the use of different film stock that conveys the special atmosphere of this sequence. It is also its stately pacing. This was only achieved on a second attempt. Having originally shot the scene exactly as planned at 17 metres (about 37 seconds), both Norstein and Skidan-Bosin were sure it was entirely wrong. So they resolved to load a full magazine of

110 Interview with Igor Skidan-Bosin, 20 April 2000, Moscow.

film for a second attempt and simply to shoot as the spirit moved them – completely spontaneously – and see what happened. The scene ended up at between 70 and 80 metres (two and a half to three minutes) which was, says Norstein, 'as it wanted to be'.[111] It also fitted perfectly into the Bach prelude Norstein had chosen to accompany the scene.

It was a scene where nothing much happened. The poet fiddled with his pen and stood looking round, his hands in his pockets ... Yet somehow every gesture seemed inspired and each moment was precious.

> But the main thing was the silence ... Just like the silence when someone doesn't answer a question immediately. When the conversation progresses slowly, punctuated by long pauses, and these pauses are not oppressive. It's as though time didn't exist in that sequence. It became spherical. With no beginning and no end.[112]

A scene had been created which did not look physically very different after the re-shoot. But, qualitatively, it was a new world: 'A world had come together in which I myself would like to rest my soul.'[113]

Now the different worlds of *Tale of Tales* and their inhabitants had been designed and shooting was progressing well. At this stage it was not yet clear how the various fragments should be ordered, but this gradually fell into place, largely by trial and error. For now the Little Wolf provided some unity by his ability to move between the worlds, but otherwise there was in general little cohesion. A more unified structure was now created by the conscious working up of various motifs to repeat in the different worlds, the main one being the green apple in the snow in the winter scene. This image resonates throughout the film in different forms, seen in the child's hand and knocked out of his hand, but now reappearing in prologue and epilogue.

Fig. 91. Norstein uses black pen-strokes to evoke wind.
[Courtesy Films By Jove]

111 He is quoting Federico García Lorca, from a letter of 12 February 1927 to Guillermo de Torre.

112 'Metafory', Part 2, *Iskusstvo kino* 8 (1994), p. 96.

113 'Dvizheniye ... Glavy iz nenapisannoi knigi', Part 1, *Iskusstvo kino* 10 (1988), p. 115.

Fig. 92 (above). Yarbusova with baby Borya. His face was given to the baby in the film.
[Photo Norstein]
Fig. 93 (top right). Yarbusova suckles baby Borya.
[Photo Norstein]

The shooting of the epilogue apple in the forest was, incidentally, another example of great ingenuity, producing magical effects from the simplest of resources. Stories flew around Moscow's animation community as to how the effect had been achieved, including the tale that an apple was placed in the street and water poured on to it from a tenth floor window. In fact, live action glycerine drops were persuaded to run down a drawn apple, which had been placed on a slope, in a path dictated by the use of vaseline.

Fig. 94 (lower right). One of the sketches Norstein did in 1968 after the birth of his son Borya, intended to be worked up as a series of paintings. The drawings show a visit of Norstein's great-aunt to view the new-born and also include dream and fantasy elements.

Another repeating motif, which echoes the apple in its form, is that rounded breast, so very full of milk. By the time the film was in production, childhood memories of Aunt Bella's breast, engorged with milk for her dead baby, had been supplemented by the magical phenomenon of the birth of Norstein's own children, Borya in 1968 and Katya in 1970. In 1968, entranced by the fact of the birth in his family, but also totally fascinated by the breastfeeding process, he had watched for hours, taken photographs and done a series of drawings intended to become paintings at some stage. Now, instead, they became another of Norstein's 'underwater' experiences to feed into this iceberg of a film. Baby Borya's face, taken from one of the photos, became the model for the suckling baby in the film [see colour plate no. 24].

Then there were the elements, which also gave a sense of unity to the film by marking scene-changes and changes of mood. One such motif was the rain, with the ubiquitous drops of water dripping off the leaves in the forest. (The drops, incidentally, were shot in live action and then printed on photographic paper, cut out and animated along with the other cut-out figures and objets.) Norstein was also interested in the portrayal of wind, in finding a way of making air and space material. He decided to render these air movements in black pen-strokes.

The film had been in production for a whole year before Goskino asked to see anything. The delivery deadline was approaching (it was supposed to be December 1978) and they wanted to be assured that the film would be in on time. Norstein told them it would (knowing full well that it would not), but he knew this was a critical moment – there was a risk of production being halted. So he exercised his right to call an extraordinary meeting of the studio's artistic council, where he showed the twenty-three or so minutes which had already been shot and explained that he needed more time to complete the film. He felt the schedule had originally been unrealistic for a film with only one animator in the team. (In fact he claims to be one of the fastest animators around, turning out an average of 150 seconds per month. Certainly his early films, each with a running time of 10 minutes and a total production schedule of seven or eight months, represent an extraordinary speed for a single animator.) The *khudsovet* were impressed by this argument but even more so by the quality of a work that resembled nothing they had ever seen before:

> Atamanov said they were obliged to give me the extension of schedule and running time that I wanted, since I was doing something quite unique. [...] He was the chairman at that time. Then Vano spoke, and Mityayev, the chief script editor – Snesarev had died by this time. And the council protected me in this way and the director of the studio could do nothing. He left the room and slammed the door. He saw I'd won. [...] He thought he had the power and suddenly he came up against another kind of power, that of the *khudsovet*. And that's how we managed to finish the film.[114]

In fact, though, the film never was entirely finished according to Norstein's conception of the work. One or two scenes were researched,

114 Interview with Yuri Norstein, 15 April 2000, Moscow.

Fig. 95 (right). Children of Maryina Roshcha, 1934. They were to serve as models for the unfilmed bird's funeral scene.

Фотография 34 год
Дети Марьиной Рощи
КН 19

Fig. 96 (below left). Valentin Zaitsev, one of Norstein's childhood friends.

Fig. 97 (below right). Drawings of children for the unfilmed scene. Norstein.

Fig. 98. Storyboard for the unfilmed scene. Norstein.

designed and storyboarded but never shot due to pressure of time. The most notable of these was a scene in which a group of children organise a funeral for a dead bird. The scene was to provide a vital link, chiming with the portrait of childhood in the winter scene, but also echoing the 'killed in action' notices of the war scenes. Again, it was crammed with reminiscences from Maryina Roshcha, the children being based on old family snapshots and one of them being modelled on Norstein's own childhood chum, Valentin Zaitsev [see colour plate no. 22, Yarbusova's sketch for the scene].

After the decision was made that these scenes had to be dropped, shooting was finished and the editing finalised, it only remained to add the sound-track. Norstein had his sights on (and got) one of Russia's finest and most celebrated actors, Alexander Kalyagin, to voice the role of the Little Wolf. A stage and screen personality, Kalyagin is probably best known in the West for his starring roles in the Nikita Mikhalkov films *Slave of Love* (*Raba lyubvi*) and *Unfinished Piece for Mechanical Piano* (*Neokonchennaya pyesa dlya mekhanicheskogo pianino*). He is now, incidentally, even more celebrated, and runs his own theatre in Moscow's New Arbat. When I interviewed him there, he was starring in *Shylock*, his new version of *The Merchant of Venice*. Norstein chose Kalyagin more on a hunch than by any scientific method. He thought the actor's eyes somewhat wolf-like. Kalyagin had previously voiced one or two cartoons – but nothing like this. He came to the recording session with no prior knowledge of the project and was shown the film,

Fig. 99 (above). Alexander Kalyagin in Shylock. *[Courtesy Etcetera Theatre]*

Fig. 100 (below). Norstein with his composer Mikhail Meyerovich. [Photo Nikolai Mikhalkovsky]

silent. He freely admits that he understood nothing. Nevertheless, Norstein managed to coax a remarkable performance out of him by asking him to think about his childhood and about his childhood fantasies. Now Kalyagin recognises the uniqueness of the whole film, including his own part in it: 'Perhaps when Yuri approached me it was not only as a great director but as a great psychologist. He understood why it should be me in that part'.[115]

For the music, Norstein turned to his regular composer Mikhail Meyerovich, with whom he had done *The Fox and the Hare*, *The Heron and the Crane* and *Hedgehog in the Fog*. Norstein himself had already decided on the major themes. The lullaby and 'Weary Sun' came from his childhood, of course. He then found the Prelude and Fugue No. 8 from Bach's *Well-Tempered Clavier,* which fitted the 'Eternity' scene like a glove, and the Mozart harpsichord concerto used for the winter scene. Interestingly, Norstein chose for his study of childhood a piece the composer had himself written at the age of 13 or 14. Yet Meyerovich's own incidental music, and his moody variations on the lullaby theme were also crucial to the film. Norstein describes Meyerovich's incidental music as 'an integral part of each pen-stroke, [which] provided a texture for the basis of the shot.'[116] A scene with a coarse, opaque surface, he said, could be followed by one in which the sound of the oboe could resolve the opacity, bringing clarity to the next scene.

Now finally, in July 1979, ideas, design, camera-work, editing and music came together. The journey Norstein had dreamed about was now complete and *Tale of Tales*, largely reflecting that journey, was also complete. But, this being Brezhnev's Soviet Union, it was far from being the end of the story. The dramas that followed could provide the material for another film.

115 Interview with Alexander Kalyagin, 20 April 2000, Moscow.

116 'Metafory', Part 2, *Iskusstvo kino* 8 (1994), p. 94.

8

The film unveiled

So what was the film that finally, in the summer of 1979, hit the screen of the Goskino cinema where all deliveries were given their final check?

If the Goskino people had been pinning their hopes on narrative content closely related to that of the shooting script, they were in for a disappointment. As we know, it could not have been more different. The film had reverted to Norstein's and Petrushevskaya's earliest ideas, as set out in the treatment. The beach story, with its poet looking for his audience and its implied indictment of philistinism and criticism of contemporary, uncultured Soviet citizens (even looking forward to the 'New Russians'), had now disappeared entirely. The criticism of contemporary life remained, but it was now housed in the entirely new winter scene – of the drunken father and vulnerable child – and its satirical tone was transmuted into a more melancholic view of a generation that has lost its purpose, its ideals.

Memories of Maryina Roshcha are now dominant again, and take their rightful place at the very beginning of the tale rather than, as in the shooting script, being summoned at the very end when the poet conjures up his own childhood memories. The plight of the contemporary poet is still there but its positioning is less prominent – and is certainly less clearly spelled out than in the somewhat schematic plotting of the shooting script. The whole of the poet's world now functions less as a criticism of the current audience for the arts than as a general plea for a more civilised future society where culture certainly plays a major role, but so also does friendship, hospitality, peace.

The Little Wolf finally emerges as the key to the whole film. Instead of arriving only at the end of the story, evoked by the lullaby as he had been in earlier versions, he now assumes multiple roles. He is the genius of the abandoned house, the spirit of a bygone age. He is the poet's longed-for reader, a perceptive reader who picks up an idea and runs with it, nurtures it. He is the structural axis of the whole film, as the only protagonist inhabiting both the world of memories and the world of the idealised future (and even making a guest appearance in the contemporary, winter scene). Finally, and crucially, his melancholic-comic persona, his burning look and his sense of longing dictate the mood of the whole piece.

As for the film's final structure, again, if Goskino had hoped for some resemblance to the linear, clear, concrete (and perhaps a bit plodding) structure of the shooting script, their hopes were vain. Yet they had been warned. Earlier, the treatment had very clearly stated that the authors did not want 'scenes with an instant interpretation'. Norstein had always said he wanted lightness and volatility and finally he found the way to introduce them. He threw out his linear narrative, relying instead on the evocation of a series of ideas – war, peace, childhood, poetry, philistinism, hospitality – there for the taking but not fully spelled out; on the creation of atmospheres; and on an editing structure that perhaps unsettled the viewer. A structure which, as critics have pointed out, itself emulated the structure of a memory, moving freely between the worlds of the film.

Here, for the sake of completeness, is the shape of the film as it was finally, and presumably with some trepidation, delivered to Goskino. But a description in words is a very, very, very poor substitute for the film itself. I do urge any reader who has not seen the film to do so as soon as possible – and to skip this chapter. But, if absolutely necessary… then start reading here.

In a brief prologue, we see an apple in the rain, a large breast with a baby suckling and a little wolf looking on, longingly. A male voice (that strikes you as strange – the owner of the voice is not identified at this point) sings the lullaby, 'The Little Grey Wolf Will Come'. The title appears, followed by the image of a large, dilapidated old wooden house.

The house is visited only briefly at this stage, as a seemingly supernatural light suddenly streams out from its depths, enticing the camera to zoom into and somehow through it, landing up in a completely different world beyond. Though its luminosity has something almost celestial about it (which is reinforced by the soundtrack changing from variations on the lullaby to the Bach Prelude and Fugue), at this first visit the new world doesn't quite live up to the heavenly ideal. In fact we see the kind of discord one might very well see in a communal flat: a harassed woman is trying to grapple with laundry, a baby and a disagreeable little girl, the latter squabbling with her playmate – who is, strangely, a bull. There is a poet in this radiant world (we know he is, from his lyre, toga and laurel wreath), but he is obviously going through a bad patch and the inspiration just will not come. He is probably not helped by his companion, a talking cat, who appears to be pushing his own suggestions as to what might constitute a good poem. But now the woman's husband, a fisherman, returns carrying a very substantial fish, and the cat stops declaiming poetry to follow the fish. The fish, still surprisingly lively, bats the cat away. Fade to black.

Back in front of the old house there is what looks like a very long table with a giant white tablecloth on it. This is lifted by the wind and carried off. We cut to a train passing, and an autumn leaf flies up in its wake. Back by the house, the makeshift line of odd tables is now revealed without its cloth. We cut to (the same?) furniture in a pile outside the house, whose windows are now being boarded up. A zoom out reveals a treadle sewing machine and some parked cars. The Little Wolf appears from behind a car and surveys his reflection in a gleaming hubcap. The piled-up furniture seems to catch fire spontaneously and the cars drive off, leaving the Wolf

Fig. 101. The fisherman with his catch. [Courtesy Films By Jove]

alone. We cut to a brief shot of some new-style, concrete housing nearby, then cut to the Little Wolf kicking autumn leaves around the yard like a kid. Now he swings on the treadle of the sewing machine. Suddenly, in long shot, the house and yard are seen under heavy snow. We zoom in towards the house and corridor – an old woman has appeared in the corridor, stoking a stove.

We cut to an outdoor dance floor, which appears to be geographically

Fig. 102. The troop train thunders by. [Courtesy Films By Jove]

Fig. 103. Little Wolf takes a look at the cars before they depart. [Courtesy Films By Jove]

adjacent to the old house. Couples dance to the war-time tango 'Weary Sun' until the record starts to jump and at each jump one of the men disappears, leaving his partner dancing alone. We see the men walking off, ghost-like, into the distance, wearing military capes. Again, changes of season, and now the women stand alone. The train – revealed to be a troop-train – passes again, illuminating the women, who catch flying scraps of paper. We see what is written on them: 'Notification', 'your husband...', 'injured', etc.

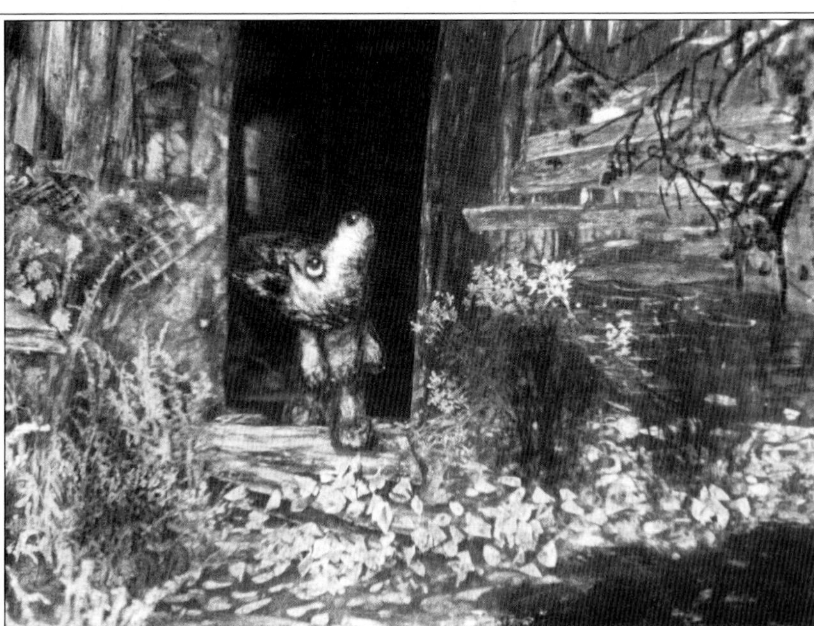

Fig. 104. Little Wolf and the autumn leaves. [Courtesy Films By Jove]

Fig. 105. Soldiers leave for the front. [Courtesy Films By Jove]

The scene ends with a solitary woman walking through a pool of light under a very puny street-lamp, the tablecloth blowing away and the troop train thundering through again, and resolves lyrically as a giant leaf lands on water and a fish appears beneath it to the accompaniment of a serene oboe motif.

We cut back to the old woman at the stove. It is still winter. We pan right and, unexpectedly, we have left the muted palette, the war-time fashions and dim lighting for a contemporary scene, rendered in saturated colours, accompanied by a Mozart harpsichord concerto on the soundtrack. A little boy with an apple stands beneath a snow-covered tree with crows in it. On a bench nearby are a couple, the man drinking vodka from the bottle. We pan back to the boy, then up into the tree where, strangely, the same little boy is sitting sharing his apple with the crows. There is some squabbling about fair shares. Meanwhile, on the bench, the man continues drinking and the woman nagging. He stands, smashes the bottle and walks off, swinging his scarf. The boy falls from the tree and is yanked away by his mother. A Napoleonic hat appears on the man's head. All three walk off in single file, but then the boy pushes aggressively in front of his mother and a Napoleonic hat falls onto his head too. They walk into whiteness. Again, a solitary woman shuffles into shot, then fades away.

We cut to the house, where the Little Wolf is sitting by the stove and the furniture is still burning. We hear, again, windows being boarded up and cars revving up. Then silence. The Little Wolf is alone. He helps himself to some potatoes and puts wood on the fire. We hear fireworks and cut to the women dancing alone. One by one, some of the men are replaced just as they had previously been removed. Now it is a returning soldier, who has lost a leg in the war, who plays the tango 'Weary Sun' on his accordion.

Intercut with this we see more of the notifications of death and injury, and we see a glass of vodka under dripping foliage and hear a victory salute in the background.

The Little Wolf sets about cooking and eating the potatoes – with some difficulty as they are too hot to hold. He sings 'Weary Sun'. A wistful look comes into his eyes and he begins to sing the lullaby. Again, light streams suddenly from the corridor in the middle of the dark house and the Little Wolf, looking round surreptitiously, moves towards the light as a double-bass takes over the lullaby theme.

Now we are back in the radiant world, with a man walking along the beach throwing stones into the sea. The soundtrack takes up the Bach Prelude and Fugue again. The walker passes the girl and bull (but stopping to skip with them for a moment), then passes the table where the fisherman is serving food to his wife and baby and the poet. But the fisherman calls the walker back to join them for dinner, which he does. The cat is contemplating a giant fish in the sea and the bull is still skipping. Finally the walker leaves, waving, and disappears over the hill. The camera rises up to watch him disappear into the distance.

Fig. 106. A solitary woman brings the winter scene to a close. [Courtesy Films By Jove]

We cut back to the table where, now, the poet's lyre, pen, inkwell and blank sheet of paper are illuminated by a candle in a jar. The Little Wolf is revealed under the table, looking across longingly at the baby, suckling at a breast. The sheet of paper begins to take on a supernatural glow. Night is falling and the fisherman's wife struggles to get her argumentative daughter indoors, while the fisherman picks up his nets and rows off into the darkness. Back at the table, the poet is still thinking hard, the Little Wolf pops his head out again and the cat, flat out on the table, extends a languid paw to extinguish the candle. The Little Wolf now grabs the paper, disappears under the table and is next seen running on a road with vehicle headlights terrifyingly close. He runs into the forest carrying his rolled paper, which has by now transmuted into a squawking bundle, a baby in fact. The traumatised Wolf shoves the baby under a bush and runs off. Thinking better of it, he returns to retrieve the infant, which by now has become a real handful, with hands and legs sticking out of the bundle in all the wrong places, crying loudly. He arrives at a bush, which seems to be his home, since a cradle is set up there in readiness. The baby is put into the cradle and rocked, while the Little Wolf sings the lullaby, at first maniacally, as the baby shows no inclination to calm down, then at the proper tempo. He tickles the baby's tummy as he sings 'and will nip you on the tum', and the baby gurgles happily.

Fig. 107. The camera rises up to watch the walker disappear into the distance. [Courtesy Films By Jove]

We zoom out, past a giant autumn leaf hanging in the rain, to an apple on the ground under the downpour.

Fig. 108. The cat sleeps, while the poet remains pensive.
[Courtesy Films By Jove]

Fig. 109. Storyboard for the theft of the paper and flight through traffic to the forest. Norstein.

Fig. 110. The Little Wolf rocks the cradle and sings his lullaby. [Courtesy Films By Jove]

To the Bach prelude, we see a final montage: the little boy in the snowy tree with his crows and the same boy under it, in the snow, with apples all round; the Little Wolf on the ground next to the apple; the soldiers marching off; the bull and the girl, skipping and squabbling; the poet; the old house, first in the snow and then under pouring rain. Finally we pan to a cobbled railway bridge and a train passes under the bridge. As the light fades a weak street-lamp comes on atop the bridge and, to an accordion version of 'Weary Sun', the credits[117] roll.

117 See appendix for full credits.

9

What's it about then, Yuri?

Reactions and repercussions 1979–1986

At first things seemed to go well. The artistic council of Soyuzmultfilm met on 2 July to receive and discuss the completed film, still at this stage entitled *The Little Grey Wolf Will Come.* The animators on the council were lavish in their praise: 'Norstein handles his instrument like a virtuoso. I consider 2 July 1979 to be a great day' (Khitruk); 'This film is a contemplation on the future of our country and of humanity as a whole ...' (Khrzhanovsky); 'Without any doubt it is a new form of animation expression... For me this film is a discovery' (Ivanov-Vano); '... a phenomenon [...] a most complex, polyphonic composition of a film [...] a summation of the experience of Soviet poetry [...] the film is world class' (Milchin); 'It has given me a feeling of surprise and a shock of joy which haven't left me' (Stepantsev).

Among the animators only Kachanov seems to have been a bit puzzled, and talks of an epigraph and a title change. (This is possibly the origin of the epigraph, found in the files after all these years, which provided the original basis for my story of Norstein's journey into the light.) Studio head Dmitri Zotov seems to have been wrong-footed by the general acclaim. He agrees with Kachanov about the epigraph and the title-change, but has to concede: 'For today we'll accept the film. The document is signed. Perhaps I'll need to add one or two concrete observations,' followed by an ambiguous remark about the problems of a large print run.

Natasha Abramova's boss at Goskino was angry and hurt at having been left out of the secret (that Norstein was actually making a different film than the agreed script). Abramova pointed out that as a Goskino employee the woman's position would have been quite untenable had Abramova confided in her, and this was accepted. She also liked the film a lot and finally agreed to defend it to her superiors.

Not only were the studio's artistic council and a Goskino chief script editor now strongly on side, but the 'mafia of decent folk' had also been at work behind the scenes and now Norstein's earlier films were suddenly under consideration for the very prestigious State Prize (*Gospremiya*). So Goskino had to pass the film for distribution. The 'mafia' seemed to have won.

Yet over at Goskino they were not feeling as relaxed about the film as the *khudsovet* was hoping. Goskino had been responsible for all aspects of cinema in the Soviet Union since 1922 (and would remain so until *glasnost*). Its script-editing department would check initial proposals, treatments and then the finished films themselves, but in the case of animation this was largely a formality. There was normally nothing seditious in a cartoon. When, however, *The Little Grey Wolf Will Come* was finally delivered, the suspicions they had been harbouring since they first, rather late in the day, asked to see the work in progress were confirmed. This was not the normal kind of cartoon they knew and loved. For one thing, it was 30 per cent longer than the agreed running time. More alarming still, the final film hardly corresponded in any respect with the treatment or the shooting script they had pored over and approved years earlier. But the most worrying aspect for these upholders of Soviet orthodoxy was that this film drove a cart and horses through the tenets of Socialist Realism, a philosophy based on optimism and clarity. They simply did not have a clue what the film was about. It did not look seditious, but who could be sure without any solid plot to make the right points?

Strangely enough, the problems they cited (not feeling able to come clean and admit they were totally in the dark) centred on the innocent-looking Little Wolf character. Goskino felt the title *The Little Grey Wolf Will Come* was somehow threatening and scary – despite the fact that generations of Russians had been successfully reared by mothers crooning these very words into their ears night after night. They had also, at one meeting, mentioned problems with the character himself. With a war going on in the background and the Little Wolf roasting potatoes in an abandoned house in the foreground – could he be a deserter? Very bad for morale, it was thought.

This finally came to a head in September, when 'Yermash, chairman of Goskino, looked at the film and said "At Soyuzmultfilm they've produced something that does not correspond at all to the principles of Socialist Realism", and he promptly cancelled the acceptance of the film.'[118] Yermash ordered the deputy head of the script-editing section of Goskino, Y. S. Avetikov, to write the following letter to the studio head. It was dated 28 September 1979:

> Having screened the delivered version of the film *The Little Grey Wolf Will Come*, written by L. Petrushevskaya and Y. Norstein and directed by Y. Norstein, the Central Script-Editing Section requests the studio:
>
> 1. To re-submit this film to Goskino USSR at a length of two reels [20 mins] as it was supposed to be according to the script and the production documents.
>
> 2. To change the name of the film to *Memories of My Childhood* which, in our opinion, corresponds better to the content of the film.

Cutting one reel out of three would have meant cutting 8 ½ minutes.

But when they showed me the letter I refused to touch the film and

118 Interview with Yuri Norstein, 15 April 2000, Moscow.

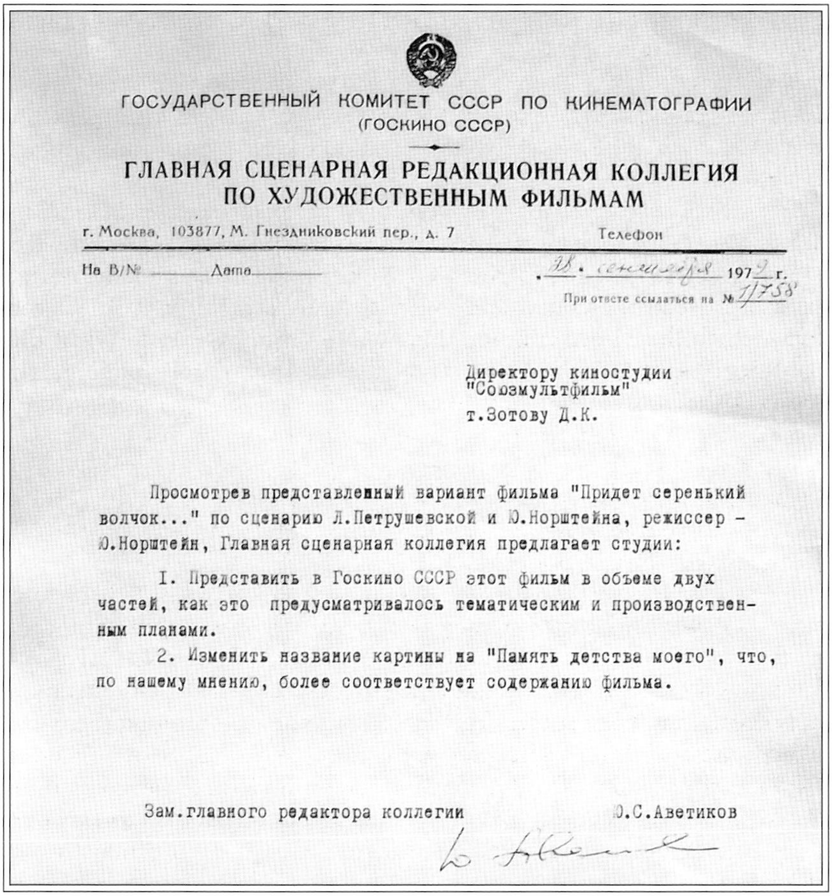

ГОСУДАРСТВЕННЫЙ КОМИТЕТ СССР ПО КИНЕМАТОГРАФИИ
(ГОСКИНО СССР)

ГЛАВНАЯ СЦЕНАРНАЯ РЕДАКЦИОННАЯ КОЛЛЕГИЯ
ПО ХУДОЖЕСТВЕННЫМ ФИЛЬМАМ

г. Москва, 103877, М. Гнездниковский пер., д. 7 Телефон

На В/№ ______ Дата ______ 28. сентября 197_ г.

При ответе ссылаться на № 1/758

Директору киностудии
"Союзмультфильм"
т.Зотову Д.К.

Просмотрев представленный вариант фильма "Придет серенький волчок..." по сценарию Л.Петрушевской и Ю.Норштейна, режиссер – Ю.Норштейн, Главная сценарная коллегия предлагает студии:

I. Представить в Госкино СССР этот фильм в объеме двух частей, как это предусматривалось тематическим и производственным планами.

2. Изменить название картины на "Память детства моего", что, по нашему мнению, более соответствует содержанию фильма.

Зам.главного редактора коллегии Ю.С.Аветиков

Fig. 111. Goskino's verdict on Tale of Tales.

wouldn't allow anyone else to touch it either. That was strange. The studio head thought he'd scare me with that bit of paper because he himself lived by those rules. That's an illustration of internal and external freedom. He thought his external freedom gave him power over people. He didn't know anything about inner freedom. He was chained to his masters. He was amazed and even frightened when I refused to change the film.[119]

Zotov's deputy, Dokuchayev, was also present when Avetikov's letter was read to Norstein. 'One other director refused to change his film', said Dokuchayev when Norstein said he would not re-edit the film, 'and he doesn't work in the cinema any more.' 'Who's that?' enquired the studio head. 'Askoldov'. [120]

Norstein immediately understood this reference (the 'mafia' saw to it that the cinema community knew everything), though the name would not become known to the general public until after May 1986 when, under *glasnost*, the Filmmakers' Union formed the Conflict Commission to investigate the banned films they found sitting on the shelves. It would then transpire that one Alexander Askoldov had been the major victim of these purges. Many of the eagerly-awaited banned films turned out, sadly, not to

119 Ibid.

120 'Snimal i "Shinel" …', *Ogonek* 43 (1988), p. 18. Norstein interviewed by Maria Dementyeva.

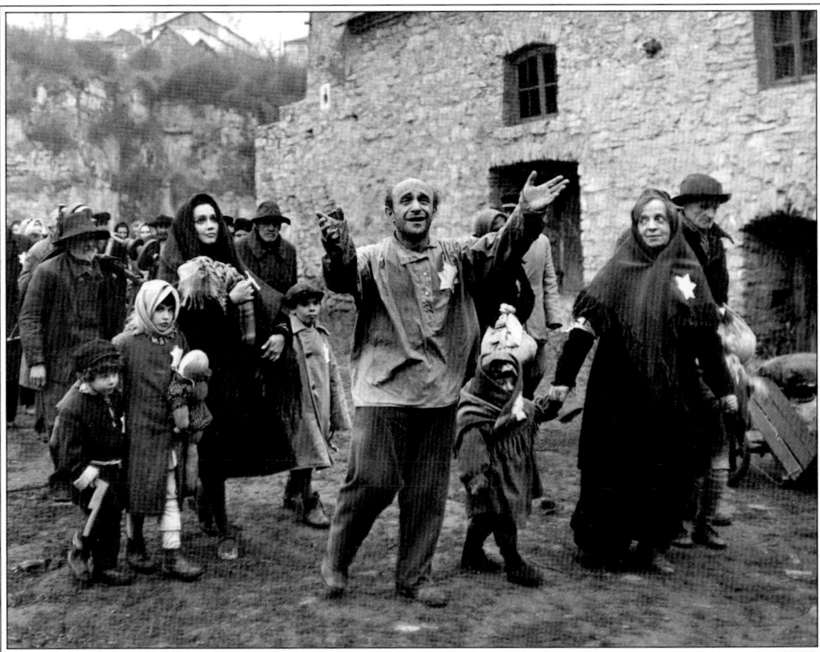

Fig. 112 (left). Natasha Abramova.
Fig. 113 (right). Alexander Askoldov's banned film Commissar, *starring Rolan Bykov.*

be very good anyway, but a very small proportion were outstanding. Most of the good directors survived the banning of one or more of their works: Klimov (all his pre-*glasnost* films were banned), Konchalovsky, Muratova, Panfilov, Bodrov, Sokurov, Smirnov for example all continued to get funding for their films and went on to highly successful cinema careers. Only Askoldov somehow managed to alienate Goskino more than the rest, to such an extent that his first film, the outstanding *Commissar* (1967), remained his last, and he was summarily dismissed for incompetence. Why was his film so much more dangerous than the rest? Primarily because it offered a sympathetic portrait of a Jewish family who give shelter to a pregnant commissar during the time of the Civil War. (The commissar, incidentally, was the Party official responsible for ideology in a military unit.)

So Norstein understood exactly what lay behind that reference to Askoldov. Financial pressure was also applied. When Natasha Abramova was told she would not receive the last payment due to her on the film, she just smiled, disconcerting them completely. This was not normal behaviour from the ranks of the 'redactors'. Presumably they were not so surprised when Norstein also remained impervious to the threat – despite the fact that, on a monthly salary of only 250 roubles, he had accumulated debts of 3,000 roubles by the end of the production.[121]

After surviving a series of such threats, Norstein went onto the offensive and organised a screening of the film to try to drum up some support. He invited film critics from the newspapers and various luminaries including Sergei Yutkevich, the much-decorated film director, teacher at VGIK, writer of film theory and many-times recipient of the State Prize. The screening was about to start when that same Dokuchayev (he of the

121 Interview with Yuri Norstein, 15 April 2000, Moscow.

Askoldov threat) discovered what was happening and came running into the room, choking with rage. He turned everyone out except Yutkevich, who was much too important to offend in this way, and critic Olga Tchaikovskaya, who managed to hide behind a column and remained while the film was screened for Yutkevich.

> Yutkevich watched the film and said: 'Yura, your team has been nominated for the State Prize. If you don't do what they're asking now you won't get the prize and you won't see your film released either. I like the film and I'll even help you re-edit it.' 'Sergei Iosifovich,' I replied, 'I have two hands, which would you like to cut off?'[122]

Stand-off, again. But then suddenly the deadlock was resolved by a complete fluke – or, rather, by the authorities' incompetence. The jury deliberating on the potential recipients of the State Prize that year had somehow not been briefed that Norstein was *persona non grata* at that moment, and they blithely went ahead and awarded him the prize. In truth, it would have looked a little odd had they not, given the long list of prizes these films had won at overseas festivals. Now, however, the authorities were in another awkward position: it did not look too good to have banned the latest work of a filmmaker whose early films had just been awarded the very prestigious State Prize.

Goskino simply had to allow the film for distribution. But they needed some kind of face-saving device:

> A week before the State Prizes were announced, I was summoned to the office of the head of the script-editing section of Goskino, Bogomolov. He was embarrassed and wouldn't look me in the eye. 'Well, Yuri Borisovich,' he said, 'we've got to get the film released somehow. What can we do?' As if it was me who'd caused this whole situation ... There was a pause. Bogomolov found a crumb or something on the table and examined it closely. He of course understood the whole thing perfectly. To cut a long story short, we agreed on a title change from *The Little Grey Wolf Will Come* to *Tale of Tales* (although I always thought the former was better and immediately set the mood).[123]

The film was allowed and the team even received their final payments eventually – though that took another decade and the advent of *glasnost*. Likewise it was only thanks to *glasnost* that the film's quality classification was changed from 1 to 'highest'.[124] That also triggered an extra payment to the crew.

Yet how could such a change in classification possibly have been refused? By that stage the film had proved to be an enormous success both domestically and internationally. It had run for over a year in the animation cinema of the Rossiya complex in Moscow. During its run, in a programme of animated shorts, it had once been taken out of the show, but had had to be put back due to popular demand. It had started its run in the middle of the programme – but half the audience had regularly stood up and left after *Tale of Tales*. So it was moved to the end. Never had any animated film been

122 *Ogonek*, ibid.

123 Ibid.

124 All films on completion were given a quality classification from 4 up to 1, with the designation 'highest' for the very best.

so successful with viewers. It was even shown from time to time on television from the early 1980s, though the TV station cut the winter scene, Norstein's core and main focus for the whole film, on the grounds that it promoted alcoholism.

Internationally it went from strength to strength in animation circles and also in Russian *émigré* circles. To them it was a breath of fresh air and a taste of freedom – a longed-for sign that things might finally be changing in their homeland. The film also conquered festival after festival, starting with the Grand Prix at Zagreb – which was the major international animation festival of that year, 1980 – and going on to win prizes at many others. In 1984 it headed the poll organised for the Los Angeles Olympiad.

Yet Norstein was still *persona non grata* at home. He was still not allowed to attend the overseas festivals where his films were showing and where there was, by this time, a throng of fans waiting to meet him. National newspapers were still 'discouraged' (read 'banned') from writing about him, even after the Olympiad of Animation poll. Mikhail Iampolski was allowed to write in the low-circulation film magazine for intellectuals, *Iskusstvo kino*, but *Sovetskaya kultura* and other large-circulation papers could not even mention the name Norstein. How times would change. When Alexander Petrov won the 2000 Oscar for best animated short film with *The Old Man and the Sea*, an Imax spectacular made in Canada with largely Canadian and some Japanese funding, plus some input from Petrov's studio in Yaroslavl, the reaction was very different. The film was based, of course, on Hemingway and seen around the world voiced in American English. This event – perhaps, given the film's international origins, less of an honour to Russia than the accolade accorded *Tale of Tales* – was reported in every publication and on every TV channel in the land. There was even a brass band awaiting Petrov on the platform when he returned to his home town after the Oscars!

Fig. 114. Francesca Yarbusova sketch for The Overcoat.

Still, in the early 1980s things were not going too badly for Norstein either. Having delivered a film, albeit in a non-standard manner, which everyone had to agree – if through gritted teeth – was good, he was now given a first tranche of funding for his next work. It was to be based on Gogol's *The Overcoat*, the tragic tale of a humble clerk whose life is ruined after he decides to invest all his pathetic savings in a new coat. Together with Yarbusova, Norstein quietly began work on this film. His name, however, was still on the forbidden list and would remain there until the advent of *glasnost*.

10

Native luggage

Norstein since 1986

After *glasnost* and *perestroika,* life changed decisively for every one of my friends in Moscow. Those who had previously scraped a living as English teachers or translators were suddenly much in demand by private clients and were now building themselves substantial dachas. Animators, however, and other creative types who had come to rely on regular, state-financed commissions for art works never liable to appeal to a mass audience, were suddenly not working and not earning. The only sure way of making a living was to get involved in a co-production with a wealthier overseas partner.

The period began well for Norstein. He was allowed to travel to various overseas film festivals and retrospectives of his work. This new visibility of the man and his films put him among the first rank of directors sought for co-production projects. He first visited the UK in 1987 for the Bristol Animation Festival and then again for a Channel 4 retrospective of his work in June 1991. At that time he stayed in my house and I went to meet him at the airport. He took an age coming out of immigration. Even taking into account the going-over that British immigration officials customarily reserved for Russian visitors, I was fearing the worst and imagined him already on a plane back to Moscow. Finally he appeared. He looked puzzled, but not as puzzled as the immigration officer who accompanied him. It seems that Norstein had been asked a question, in English, which he had not understood. He had attempted, for the first and last time in his life, to respond in English. 'I have no luggage,' he averred, 'only my native luggage.' This of course had led to searches in the baggage hall until it had been realised that Norstein had been referring to his failure to master any foreign languages.

I mention this because Norstein had inadvertently hit upon the perfect summation of one of his major character traits. He does indeed carry round with him an enormous amount of native luggage, and this has been in evidence throughout the *débâcle* over *The Overcoat*. Soyuzmultfilm had accepted the proposal in 1980 and provided funding, and production had started. Again, the winning team of Petrushevskaya and Norstein had written the script. The first three years were bedevilled by stops and starts and changes in direction. There had been a long delay while Norstein

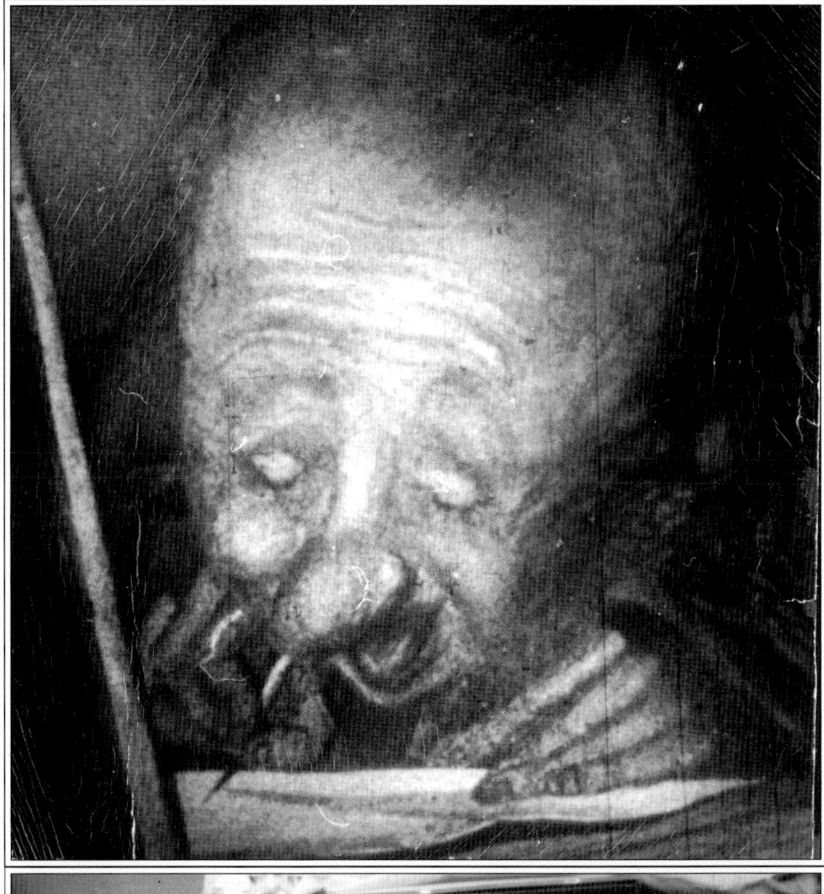

Fig. 115. The Overcoat: *Akaki Akakievich settles down to a calligraphy session.*

Fig. 116. Norstein and Zhukovsky in 1985. [Photo Herz Frank]

fought, unsuccessfully, to get cameraman Zhukovsky's salary raised. Production proper had started in 1983 and Norstein, Yarbusova and Zhukovsky worked flat out from then on. There had been some excitement when a 1½ -minute scene had been shot and turned out to run 16 minutes. As with the 'Eternity' sequence in *Tale of Tales*, the scene seemed to have taken on a life of its own. Akaki Akakievich's return home and settling down to a calligraphy session had metamorphosed into a detailed character study. The studio heads, paying more attention this time, raised hell, but to no avail of course. Now, however, in mid-1986, the film's delivery date had arrived but the film was not complete. Since the three had been working flat-out for three years, animating at an amazingly fast rate for such a tiny team, one can only assume that the original schedule was, as for *Tale of Tales*, not worked out properly.

Not only was the film not complete but, having started out as a two-reel (20-minute) proposal, the planned film had now become feature-length. In the old days filmmakers were often late in delivery and it was not unknown for running times to be extended during production. But, come what may, they would simply carry on until the film was finished. Now under *perestroika* the studio was better organised and Norstein's studio space had been booked out, after the period allocated to him, to another director. Norstein and colleagues were unceremoniously removed and the multiplane animation stand dismantled until it could be reassembled elsewhere.

But where? When the studio failed to come up with any alternative premises in Moscow, offers started rolling in from overseas production companies, sympathetic to Norstein's plight and of course anxious to have their names associated with the next Norstein masterpiece! Organisations in Canada, Belgium, France, the USA, Japan and Czechoslovakia all at different times offered Norstein premises and funding. But he refused to go. For Norstein, of course, making a film is not just a matter of turning up at the studio every morning. For him those endless phone conversations in the middle of the night that Muscovites all indulge in are part of the inspiration, as are the nasty incidents one may encounter in crowds pushing to get into the crowded metro. Everything, in fact, constitutes irreplaceable 'native luggage' to Norstein: all the sights, sounds and smells of his home city. And then there is the 'grazed elbow' factor.

> I would of course make the film, in a professional manner. But there would only be professionalism. There wouldn't be any passion, there'd be no grazed elbow in it ... Once as a child I fell off my bike and grazed my elbow. [...] I couldn't feel the rest of my body at all, only the elbow. And it's like that with work – you should only work with this injured part. All the rest is meaningless. And you only get that feeling at home. It would certainly disappear if you went abroad. And the result would be nothing more than a very pleasant film. It seems to me that it's better to have mistakes in the film (some of the best films have mistakes in them), but the mistakes must be your own and they must hurt. That's why I can't leave. [...]
>
> Even if I leave Moscow for a week I suffer terribly ... [125]

125 'Snimal i "Shinel" ...', *Ogonek* 43 (1988), p. 17. Norstein interviewed by Maria Dementyeva.

Fig. 117. Native luggage: Norstein takes a daily dip, even when the outside temperature is 20°below zero. [Photo Kosei Miya]

Fig. 118. Native luggage: After a few drinks, the singing of Russian songs becomes a very serious business. With Edward Nazarov and Mikhail Aldashin at the Zagreb Animation Festival, 2002. [Photo Clare Kitson]

Meanwhile the search for premises in Moscow continued. Moscow city council's help was enlisted, but they could find nothing with the 140 square metres needed for the production. At around this time there was a proposal from the Cinema Museum to convert a two-storey house in which Tarkovsky had once lived, near Dobryninskaya metro station, to a museum devoted to Tarkovsky, his teacher Mikhail Romm and fellow-student and cult writer, actor and filmmaker Vasily Shukshin. The lower floor was to be offered to Norstein to house the production of *The Overcoat*. But the plan came to nothing. Funds could not be found for this ambitious refurbishment scheme.

Norstein's relationship with Soyuzmultfilm continued to worsen until, in August 1989, he decided to leave, amidst great acrimony. However, salvation appeared to be at hand, from two very different but seemingly complementary sources. Firstly, French Minister of Culture Jack Lang had attended the Annecy Animation Festival that year, had seen Norstein's films and learned of his situation. Lang determined to use substantial funds from his special budget for collaboration with Eastern Europe in order to help Norstein finish his film in Russia. At the same time Soyuzmultfilm's interest in the project was bought up by the Bykov Foundation, an organisation for the production and promotion of family-oriented cinema, set up by the much-loved Russian actor-director Rolan Bykov. French TV channel La Sept-Arte, which had done much to promote Norstein's work in France, now came on board, and they brought in an animation producer who was experienced in international co-productions. Norstein was set up in a new studio which was to be equipped as part of the co-production agreement and everything seemed set to proceed smoothly. It did not, however. Amid rising anger and accusations on both sides all collaboration came to a dramatic halt. So did all funding for the film.

As this book goes to press, Norstein is still soldiering on with the project, but he needs funds to live on, to pay the studio rent and to pay his small band of collaborators. Since the French *débâcle*, he refuses even to consider offers of finance from the West. He has, however, received some funding from Russian sponsors including a bank. But not enough, so production is regularly interrupted for short trips to animation schools abroad where he can earn a fee to plough back into the film. Likewise, he suspends production to make commercials (including a very charming series of sugar ads) and he was recently kept from *The Overcoat* for over a year while working on a lavish and technically breathtaking title sequence for an entirely pedestrian children's TV series, *Good Night Kids* (*Spokoinoi nochi malyshi*) [see colour plate no. 13]. Norstein's art director on this sequence once found me sitting in the studio kitchen, somewhat aghast, watching this programme on television. 'Now you know our shame!' he said, with grim humour.

But it is not only the need for funds that keeps Norstein from *The Overcoat*. It is also an almost obsessive perfectionism which meant that, for example, having completed and delivered in 2003 a 1½-minute segment for a portmanteau film based on a Japanese poem, which was put out on

Fig. 119. Norstein working on The Overcoat. *[Photo Nikolai Vasilkov]*

Fig. 120. An anonymous exterior houses Norstein's current studio. [Photo Clare Kitson]

Fig. 121. Class 2B, School No. 606, Maryina Roshcha, with teacher Varvara Gregoryevna, in 1949. Norstein is second from left in the front row.

DVD, he then continued, on his own initiative, making his own – longer and more perfect – 'director's cut'.

Norstein is still revered by the public, especially for *Tale of Tales* and for *Hedgehog in the Fog*, which is a part of all Russians' childhood. An exhibition at Moscow's Cinema Museum celebrating the 20th anniversary of *Tale of Tales* attracted visitors of all ages, all equally spell-bound by what they had seen. One entry in the exhibition's visitors' book says: 'We are staggered by your film. It makes us look at life differently.' Another: 'This filmmaker has reached into the depths of our culture and our soul, has awakened the goodness in us, given us hope and a sense to our life.' Another, by a 9 year-old, says 'Your films are mysterious and strange and we really want you to make another one.' A group of Norstein's class-mates (class of '57) from School No. 606, Maryina Roshcha, wrote in the book: 'Thank you for letting us plunge back into our youth.'

The film is now seen regularly on television, in its entirety, despite the drunk in the winter scene. It tends to be shown on very special occasions, such as the celebrations marking the 50th anniversary of the end of the war, when there was a minute's silence, followed by *Tale of Tales*. It also sometimes gets shown when there are national tragedies, such as the murder of the progressive and very popular member of parliament Galina Starovoitova.

Yet despite massive public respect and affection, the philistines are still there in positions of power and, sadly, Norstein is still *persona non grata*. The people in power are no longer ruled by ideology but by commerce and Norstein, still the poet who refuses to compromise, seems less well-adapted to fight the power of money and new business practices than he was when Communist ideology and administration were the enemy.

This is not surprising given his background, which constitutes a large part of that 'native luggage'. A childhood under Stalin taught him resilience and self-reliance; his teenage years under Khrushchev encouraged independent thought; and the majority of his adult life under Brezhnev refined his inclination to obstinacy and his talent (shared with the rest of the population) for obfuscation. Nothing in Norstein's background had prepared him for a working relationship in which plans, budgets and schedules are accurately prepared and then rigorously adhered to. The Communist system had never dealt in finite sums of money or periods of time and Communist-era bosses were never of the kind that one would confide in, trust or regard as a valued partner.

It has to be said, however, that such bosses were also in short supply in the early days of *perestroika* so even the most collaboratively-inclined artist would have found it hard to work alongside them. Furthermore, now that the Soviet economy was no longer in a position to print money, even the most benevolent studio head would have found his means much reduced and the studio's functioning dependent on servicing foreign series and on co-productions. Even if Norstein had been a team-player ready to compromise, and even had he encountered the most enlightened studio head in the world, it would have been hard to make a project like *The Overcoat* in

Fig. 122. Inside Norstein's studio. [Photo Clare Kitson]

the early days of *perestroika*. *Tale of Tales*, much as it ran counter to Brezhnev-period aesthetic norms was, ironically, very much a product of the lackadaisical administration of its era. It would be impossible for Norstein to repeat the experience in Russia today.

Norstein has made his journey into the luminosity of the creative world. An extraordinary effort of will has brought him through his country's darkest times and the particular tribulations suffered by Jewish citizens, and out of a working-class into an intellectual milieu. As well as accumulating a sizeable collection of trophies (very few of which, of course, actually reached Norstein), he has also managed to remain a thorn in the side of the Moscow cinema authorities, which is perhaps in Norstein's terms the greatest accolade of all. If his next magnum opus is progressing slowly – well, he and his colleagues are nevertheless talking and thinking about it the whole time. It is a far cry from Maryina Roshcha and the daily struggles for basic survival.

But like his alter ego the Little Wolf Norstein spends a lot of time in the darkness too. Darkness, figuratively speaking, because some of the jobs he has to take on to keep *The Overcoat* production going is hack-work and certainly not to be confused with high art. Physically, too, his studio (which is also now his home), while it has none of the privations of a 1940s or 1950s communal flat, does remind me strangely of the house in *Tale of Tales*, with its dark central corridor. One door off this corridor leads to the windowless camera room, another to an equally windowless cubicle housing an editing table and a third to a spacious studio where artwork is produced and where, also, visitors are housed. When I stayed there on one occasion, there were two of us. Norstein's producer, who lives in St Petersburg, had got there first so she had a little cubby-hole with screens around it. I was sleeping out in the middle of the studio, but nobody seemed to find this at all odd. I got the impression that others could also have been accommodated in a similarly relaxed, and communal, manner.

Another door off the corridor leads to Norstein's kitchen, which is not particularly luminous but nevertheless witnesses an almost constant re-enactment of *Tale of Tales*' 'Eternity' scene. Crowds of friends (and, I am sure, a few strangers who happen to be passing) are fed and watered. A lot of improvisation takes place if there is not much in the fridge. Red wine, if available, is offered. Vodka is always on the menu. Conversations last long into the night … .

Tale of Tales

Proposal for a 20-minute animated film

This is to be a film about memory.

Do you remember how long the days were when you were a child?

Each day stood alone and we lived for that day – tomorrow would be there for tomorrow's pleasures.

All truths were simple, everything new amazed us, and friendship and comradeship stood above all else.

That constant postponing of life until tomorrow, a practice that besets many of us as we get older, that hit or miss sort of life, that friendship that isn't really friendship, that joy we don't recognise as joy – in the sun, the snow, the wind, a walk, a smooth, well-washed plate, dogs, cats ... – may we be spared any such passive sitting-out of our fate.

But that's not what the film is about.

The film will feature a poet in the main role, yet the poet does not necessarily have to appear on screen – perhaps his poem could appear, a poem such as that by Nazım Hikmet, a poem we know in Russia as 'Tale of Tales':

> We stand over the water –
> the sun, the cat, the plane tree and I, and our fate.
> The water is cool,
> the plane tree tall,
> the sun shines,
> the cat dozes,
> I write verses.
> Praise God, we are alive!
> The water's shimmer strikes us in the face –
> the sun, the cat, the plane tree and me, and our fate.[126]

A cat is to be seen in the film, a loving creature with a retentive memory. And there will be a single boot, without its pair, found by children in the rubbish. Who could have put it there, a new boot, its sole intact? And that birch tree stump which, as Tvardovsky says, in spring 'will break out in a pink foam', and all the neighbourhood butterflies, beetles and wasps,

126 Here I have translated the poem as it appears, slightly misquoted, in the proposal. Compare chapter 5, which has a translation of the actual text of the published Russian version of the poem.

thin after the winter, will fly to the feast. It will rain, and the rain will feed the earth, fill the boot and the birch stump and wash down the cobbled road. At the end of the street twilight will fall and linger long ...

Washing on lines, a bull with a ring through its nose, full of terrible, destructive passions; grandpa in his village with only one leg; our neighbour, back from the war having suffered the same fate ... Our neighbour with one boot ...

All this can be organised into a simple but very special story, opening up like a concertina, widening out and then finally squeezing down to one simple sound: 'Life'.

For our childhood was at the end of the war, and we must always remember that happiness is each new day of peace. Each new day.

L. Petrushevskaya
Y. Norstein

Tale of Tales

Treatment for an animated film

Director: Y. Norstein
Moscow, 1976

I don't know how it was down your way, but where we lived every evening, every summer evening – even after rain, when the sun was setting behind the clouds and a smell of wet foliage hung over the wet earth – every quiet evening when the weather was fine they used to play the tune 'Weary Sun' in the park.

At that time, after the war, it was quiet in the evenings and 'Weary Sun' used to float without interference, pure and unsullied, through the trees in the park, straight in through windows, open during the summer, to where mothers were laying tables. But people got fed up with 'Weary Sun', so much so that, thirty years later, I've searched high and low for the record and can't find it – it wore out its welcome during the war ...

I heard so much of that tune that it has been sounding in my ears ever since and bringing back memories of how my Mum was young then, with shoulder-pads and funny felt boots, and how Tolya the bandit lived across the yard, 12 years old and disabled, a poor child of the war. Now he'd get washed and fed, but then he terrified us when his gang walked around the yard with him, its squat little leader, limping – for his right leg had been mutilated in an explosion ...

If only we could go back now to that poor childhood, sustained by ration cards, to that long corridor, to the sunny Sunday yard – without grown-ups, for they're asleep – where the children all gather ...

If only we could look now, with different eyes, at the homeland of our childhood, at that cramped yard, where the earth was so trampled that the grass only pierced a way through around the edges, where the wind-blown earth floor glistened in the sun, glistened with tiny shards of glass – where did all those different-coloured bits of glass come from in those days?

And where did all that happiness come from in those days?

All that happiness …

But we've already lived out that happiness. We've done all our running under the summer rain. We've had our fill of it. For us now, no more running, no more jumping, no more skipping.

It's hard to believe people practise sport for their health, running stupidly, dripping with sweat …

But the film won't be about that. We don't want to take anyone back to the land of their childhood to taunt them along the lines of: Look at you then and look at you now … Look at that boy with dirty hands, clutching a slice of black bread spread with sugar (he's got sugar on his nose too), and look at him now, quite a different person. How he's changed! Don't you want to change back? You can, you know; it wouldn't cost you anything. Remember all that happiness!

No, the film isn't about that.

In the film childhood will be there as part of an enormous and magnificent life of the whole world at all times. What we need to grasp is not so much that children hold the secret of happiness – but that we also hold that secret. Each of us has this, his own, secret, but we often keep it secret from ourselves …

The script should not feature scenes with an instant interpretation such that the reader nods his head after each turn thinking: yes, got it, I've got what they mean by that.

We want the whole film to say THIS:

People, you are splendid.

Childhood is a splendid time.

Thunder – I love thunder.

It's evening. Someone is coming. You can hear his footsteps – it's an everyday thing. Footsteps in the darkening air. Another person walks towards him. Tap tap. Someone like me. He greets me. But I don't know him. He walks on.

A splendid human being has passed me by.

And I am a poet.

Everything I see, everything I hear touches me to the depths of my soul.

I am a sensitive creature, lacerated by my feelings. My workplace is the square, the street, the beach. The people. It is they who, without knowing it, dictate to me my themes and sometimes whole phrases. Not to mention the colours – I just paint them from nature.

So here I am, sitting in the square.

This is, as I've already mentioned, my place of work.

So what if it's uncomfortable. I've already accepted that it will be crowded. Crowds, crowds, crowds…

And I sit with my lyre, or stand wearing a laurel wreath, and twang my lyre. Or, put more simply, I write – and they are free to take what I have just written, take it away from the dust and the heat.

I've accepted that – it's fine if my poems disappear into the gaping maw of the crowd.

But – this is strange – they don't disappear. They just lie around under everyone's feet. Someone has torn a little bit off and stuck it on his nose. Someone else is using it to clean out a fish ...

That doesn't mean that you have before you a parable entitled 'The Rejected Poet'.

Simply, every poet – every one, for this is a peculiarity of poets – during the course of his development goes through a stage entitled 'And who are you, where's it written that you're a poet?'

New-born poets are ignored – openly, persistently and even somehow polemically. Fanatically. 'That chap might be a poet too, but he doesn't get under everyone's feet, try to draw attention to himself ... And he doesn't sigh ostentatiously – he sighs to himself.'

But this one is writing things, reading them, tearing them up ... Strumming his lyre. Mumbling.

A lot of people are getting irritated.

But I am a poet all the same. I see each one of you. Your pain is my pain. You, for example, solitary tourist with a tripod, where are you off to? Tourists move in groups, but you're alone ... There's nothing worse than a solitary tourist, especially with a camera. There will be photos – all views, views, views. And you won't appear anywhere in the photos ...

No, but this solitary tourist, as it happens, is carrying a tripod. He'll set up the camera, set the delayed action shutter release and will photograph himself – always himself, himself. Against a background of rocks, against the sea ... Lying down, sitting, standing ... So then, you poor tourist, there won't be so much as a single view to be seen in your photos, only you. Poor chap, poor fellow. My heart bleeds for you. I'll write some verses about you.

Poor chap, poor fellow – but look! He doesn't feel too bad. He's pinned my little poem to the sand with the leg of his tripod ...

And now I write my greeting to someone else.

This one is lying down and has buried himself in the sand. He has gone off some distance from everyone else. But he hasn't forgotten them and has, for their edification, drawn a circle round himself: no entry, it warns.

O you, who have walked away from society but are keeping close watch lest someone else should follow: This place is already taken!

And my poem, my slip of paper has gently floated over to him and landed on that place in the sand under which his heart should be.

And at last there's a reader, my reader, a constant reader of all – any – scraps of paper, advertisements, booklets. He will understand me. He will put on a pair of 5 dioptre reading glasses, will understand and evaluate.

There he goes, peering short-sightedly. He pokes his head in front of the lens and peeps through it at the Solitary Tourist preparing to take a photo; and he steals a glance at the Man Buried in the Sand, in his circle.

He will catch sight of my missives, read them and sprout wings.

He'll have wings!

He will summon everyone to share this joy and will have the reading masses, as they're called, following behind him.

He will show everyone: Look, I've grown wings!

Let's go. There's something there for all of you in the verses!

And indeed there is!
This man has a vision of an enormous car.
He sees himself flinging open the car door.
And sitting down on the seat.
But my goodness, how small he is! He can't reach the steering wheel! Or the pedals!
Can it be that he isn't grown up enough yet for such a car?
He convinces himself that he is indeed big enough, he puffs himself up and sits in the car, full of pride.
But his pride leaves him – through his ears, let's say.
He stops up one ear, then the other – with corks.
Then a polite traffic policeman says something to him.
But his ear is stopped up!
And if he takes the stopper out, his pride will escape.
But he mustn't drive off, he must understand what's being said …
Otherwise he'll be breaking the law!
Meanwhile the Solitary Tourist also has a vision – that he is getting married.
The bride is blonde and wears a veil.
They are walking down an enormous and very grand flight of steps.
The only thing is, he's in his swimming trunks …
At the bottom of the steps they are met by people who, it turns out, want to give him some sort of a badge. A badge acknowledging distinction in getting married, perhaps.
But there's nowhere to pin it. Not on his swimming trunks!
And the Man Buried in the Sand, with the circle round him that everyone is trying to penetrate, imagines that he is a bull! And with a roar he leaps out of the sand, scaring everybody away.
And a man drinking beer, with his hand at his side, imagines he is a bugler.
And that everyone at the beer stall has changed. Some, downing the last drop, are buglers and others, bending down and just beginning to drink from their tankards, are saxophonists.
And the short-sighted man, fluttering along, is dropping slips of paper …
The Bull catches one on his horn.
He is obliged to read it, as it's hanging over his eye.
He lies down and, propping himself up on one elbow, reads.
He gazes thoughtfully into the distance.
There, in the distance, on a shell, a cow is approaching through the surf.
She stands in a Botticelli-style pose.
But – she is chewing.
She floats past.
The Bull leaps into action and rushes off, his head in a spin. He runs straight into someone's skipping rope and skips frantically …
The fluttering Reader has dropped a sheet of paper down to the Poet as well, and he reads it through anxiously …
And he sees buildings round a yard. It is evening and lights burn at the windows. A wavering voice carries from a gramophone on a window sill, a soldier with a crutch is sitting on a bench, two young ladies with perms are dancing and a barber is standing at the door of his little lair …

There, in that yard, the post-war summer is never ending and the record 'Weary Sun', having given honourable service throughout the war, is still reminding us over and over …
The Bull is there too – skipping…
Our Car Owner is also there – leading the car by a rope …
A woman there is singing a lullaby to a child.

Baby baby rock a bye
On the edge you mustn't lie
Or the little grey wolf will come
And will nip you on the tum
And will nip you on the tum
Tug you off into the wood
Underneath the willow root [127]

The baby is twisting and turning, staring into the darkness …
It's dark, it's dark, the forest is dark and there, sitting under a bush – a brittle willow bush – is the Little Wolf…
He gives the impression of sitting there clothed, with upturned collar and arms in sleeves…
His eyes are burning!
Lonely, lonely Little Wolf …
Evidently a droplet has fallen from the tree above; he shakes his ear and looks up.
Then he turns his ardent gaze back to the baby…
Pitter-patter…
Rain.
The outlines of houses round the yard, lights at the windows, rain all over the world, thunder are all being washed away…
The soldier leaves the courtyard on one leg, wearing one boot…
Another, similar, boot is left standing, alone in the rain …
The Tourist with the tripod leaves the beach, soaked. The Reader's wings are drooping…
The Poet remains, sitting alone in the rain.
Everyone has gone.
But it seems to the Poet that someone is calling him.
Someone is waving to him from under a sort of awning.
A fisherman is sitting there and another chap.
A nice chap that nobody knows, the kind that always turns up at supper tables you get invited over to.
The Poet sits at the table. Bread. Wine. A butterfly perches on the edge of a glass.
The low evening sun peeks out from behind the clouds.
The world is drying out – only the boot remains full of water. The Cat comes along and drinks from it.
The Little Wolf creeps in under the awning and takes for himself a sheet of verse, rolls it up into a tube and, looking round stealthily, carries it off into the dark forest …

127 Traditional lullaby translated by Gaby and Vitaly Yerenkov.

He carries it, clutched to his bosom, and wraps it up more snugly.
He sings a lullaby to the bundle he carries and glances down at it …
Two bright eyes are shining up at him …
The Little Wolf is carrying a baby.
The butterfly is flapping expansively above them, a drop of wine on its proboscis …

Baby baby rock a bye, on the edge you mustn't lie …

We hear the main song of the film, the lullaby.

Or the Little Grey Wolf will come and will nip you on the tum …
Tug you off into the wood, underneath the willow root …

The tipsy butterfly is dancing above their heads …
The Little Wolf is carrying a baby, carrying the happiness he'd dreamed of …
He carries it to his home and there we see – for this is no Big Bad Wolf and he won't be gobbling anyone up – a little cradle.
The Little Wolf puts the baby to bed and tucks a blanket in around it …
He looks cautiously out of the window, then draws the curtain.
He sings in a deep voice:

On the edge you mustn't lie!

THE END
L. Petrushevskaya
Y. Norstein

Tale of Tales Credits

Screenplay	L. Petrushevskaya Y. Norstein
Director/Animator	Y. Norstein
Design	F. Yarbusova
Camera	I. Skidan-Bosin
Voice of the Little Wolf	A. Kalyagin
Composer	M. Meyerovich
Sound	B. Filchikov
Music taken from works by	J. S. Bach and W. A. Mozart
Editor	N. Treshcheva
Script Editor	N. Abramova
Producer	G. Kovrov

Time Line:

From Norstein's birth to completion of *Tale of Tales*

Year	Age	Personal and animation landmarks	USSR
1941		Born, Andreyevka, Penza province.	Germany invades USSR.
1942	1		
1943	2	Family moves back to Moscow suburb of Maryina Roshcha.	
1944	3		
1945	4		Soviet troops into Berlin. End of war in Europe.
1946	5		Zhdanov launches attacks on 'individualist' writers. Churchill's 'Iron Curtain' speech – the Cold War has begun.
1947	6		
1948	7	Starts at junior school. Given book of Russian painters.	Solomon Mikhoels murdered by Ministry of State Security.
1949	8		
1950	9		
1951	10	Moves from junior to senior school. Starts reading adventure stories and English and Russian classics.	Start of the 'doctors' plot' affair.

Year	Age	Personal and animation landmarks	USSR
1952	11	Few months of extra-curricular art lessons – dismissed. Father dismissed from job, forced to take on far harder work, some distance from Moscow.	
1953	12		Death of Stalin. Succeeded by Khrushchev.
1954	13		Publication of Ehrenburg's *The Thaw*.
1955	14		
1956	15	Death of father. Starts attending art school two days per week. Discovers Japanese poetry.	20th Party Congress – Khrushchev denounces Stalin. Dresden Gallery exhibition. Soviet troops into Hungary.
1957	16		Release of Kalatozov's *The Cranes Are Flying*.
1958	17	Fails entrance exams to fine arts institutes. Job in furniture factory. Continues at art school in evenings.	Pasternak forced to turn down Nobel prize.
1959	18	Joins vocational animation course at Soyuzmultfilm studio.	Release of Chukhrai's *Ballad of a Soldier* and Bondarchuk's *Destiny of a Man*.
1960	19		
1961	20	Graduates from Soyuzmultfilm animation course and becomes animator at studio proper. Discovers Latin American poetry.	Gagarin first man in space.
1962	21	Khitruk makes *The Story of One Crime* – Soyuzmultfilm's first adult-oriented cartoon. Norstein registered as artist/animator category 3.	Publication of Solzhenitsyn's *One Day in the Life of Ivan Denisovich*. Khrushchev visits exhibition of experimental work of the Moscow branch of the Union of Soviet Artists — unimpressed. Beginning of end of the Thaw. Cuban missile crisis.
1963	22		Publication of Solzhenitsyn's *Matrena's Home*.

Year	Age	Personal and animation landmarks	USSR
1964	23	Works as animator on Ivanov-Vano's *The Left-Handed Craftsman* (aka *The Steel Flea*).	Publication of first volume of Eisenstein's *Selected Works*. Triumvirate of Brezhnev, Kosygin and Podgorny replaces Khrushchev.
1965	24		Khutsiyev's *I Am Twenty* released in cut form.
1966	25	At Soyuzmultfilm Khrzhanovsky makes *Once There Was a Man Called Kozyavin* and Khitruk makes *Man in the Frame*, both critical of bureaucracy. Norstein registered as artist/puppet-animator category 2.	Tarkovsky's *Andrei Rublev* completed (but held back from domestic distribution until 1971).
1967	26	Marries Francesca Yarbusova. Moves away from Maryina Roshcha. Animates on Kachanov's *The Mitten.* Starts work (as co-director with Arkadi Tyurin) on *25th – the First Day*. Meets Lyudmila Petrushevskaya.	Askoldov's *Commissar* completed and banned.
1968	27	Son Borya born. Khrzhanovsky makes *The Glass Harmonica* – banned.	Brezhnev dominating the triumvirate. Soviet troops into Czechoslovakia.
1969	28	Registered artist/puppet-animator category 1. Director on *Children and Matches.* Assistant director on Ivanov-Vano's *The Seasons.* Petrushevskaya starts writing fiction.	
1970	29	Daughter, Katya, born. Family moves to Belyayevo. Co-directs on Ivanov-Vano's *Battle by the Kerzhenets.*	Solzhenitsyn awarded Nobel Prize for Literature.
1971	30		
1972	31		
1973	32	Directs *The Fox and the Hare.*	
1974	33	Directs *The Heron and the Crane.* Mayakovsky project aborted. Petrushevskaya banned from publication.	Sozhenitsyn expelled from USSR.

Year	Age	Personal and animation landmarks	USSR
1975	34	Directs *Hedgehog in the Fog*.	Tarkovsky's *Mirror* released. Andrei Sakharov awarded Nobel Peace Prize.
1976	35	Registered director category 1. *Tale of Tales* treatment accepted. Development work started.	
1977	36	Registered director category 'highest'. *Tale of Tales* on hold. Animates on *One Day B.C.E.* and Part 1 of Khrzhanovsky's *Pushkin Trilogy*. *Tale of Tales* into production.	
1978	37		
1979	38	*Tale of Tales* completed. Norstein's early films win State Prize.	Soviet invasion of Afghanistan.

Yuri Norstein Filmography

1962 *Zhivye tsifry* (*Living Numbers*), drawn, 9:31 min, animator (dir. R. Davydov)

Dve skazki (*Two Tales*), drawn, 16:18 min, animator (dir. L. Amalrik)

Kto skazal miyau? (*Who Said Miaow?*), puppets, 9:12 min, animator (dir. V. Degtyarev)

Vnimaniye, v gorode volshebnik (*Look Out, There's a Magician in Town*), (live action feature with a puppet-animated section) 80:00 min, animator (dir. V. Bychkov), for Belarusfilm with animated section by Soyuzmultfilm

1963 *Skazka o starom kedre* (*Tale of the Old Cedar*), puppets and live action, 18:18 min, animator (dir. V. Degtyarev)

Mister Twister, flat puppets, 16:12 min, animator (dir. A. Karanovich)

Moskvichok (*The Little Moskvich Motor Car*), puppets, 7:54 min, animator (dir. I. Boyarsky)

1964 *Levsha* (*The Left-Handed Craftsman*), drawn and cut-out, 42:00 min, animator (dir. I. Ivanov-Vano)

Moskovskiye novosti (*Moscow News*), puppets, 8:06 min, animator (dir. I. Boyarsky)

1965 *Kak odin muzhik dvukh generalov prokormil* (*How One Peasant Fed Two Generals*), cut-out, 22:58 min, animator (dir. I. Ivanov-Vano, V. Danilevich)

Kanikuly Bonifatsiya (*Bonifacio's Holiday*), drawn, 20:24 min, animator (dir. F. Khitruk)

1966 *Moi zeleny krokodil* (*My Green Crocodile*), puppets, 9:12 min, animator (dir. V. Kurchevsky)

Podi tuda – ne znayu kuda (*Probably That Way – I Don't Know*), cut-out with some puppets, 55:36 min, animator (dir. I. Ivanov-Vano, V. Danilevich)

1967 *Varezhka* (*The Mitten*), puppets, 10:18 min, animator (dir. R. Kachanov)

	Nu i Ryzhik! (*Good Old Ginger!*), puppets, 10:24 min, animator
1968	*Legenda o zlom velikane* (*Legend of the Wicked Giant*), puppets, 10:00 min, animator (dir. I. Ivanov-Vano, V. Danilevich)
	Ostorozhno, shchuka! (*Careful – Pike!*), puppets, 18:54 min, animator (dir. I. Ufimtsev, M. Kamenetsky)
	25e – pervy den (*25th – the First Day*), cut-out, 8:05 min, co-director, co-scriptwriter and co-art director (with Arkadi Tyurin), animator
1969	*Zhadny Kuzya* (*Greedy Kuzya*), puppets and live action, 10:48 min, animator (dir. I. Ufimtsev, M. Kamenetsky)
	Skazka pro kolobok (*Tale of a Pie*), puppets, 10:00 min, animator (dir. N. Chervinskaya)
	Vremena goda (*The Seasons*), puppets, 9:03 min, assistant director (to I. Ivanov-Vano), animator
	Babushkin zontik (*Grandma's Umbrella*), puppets, 9:03 min, animator (dir. L. Milchin)
	Deti i spichki (*Children and Matches*), cut-out, 6:00 min, director, animator
1970	*Pismo* (*The Letter*), puppets, 9:36 min, animator (dir. R. Kachanov)
	Bobry idut po sledu (*Beavers Follow the Track*), puppets, 18:36 min, animator (dir. M. Kamenetsky)
1971	*Secha pri Kerzhentse* (*Battle by the Kerzhenets*), cut-out, 10:12 min, co-director (with I. Ivanov-Vano), animator
	Malchik i myachik (*The Little Boy and the Ball*), puppets, 10:00 min, animator (dir. V. Danilevich)
	Cheburashka, puppets, 20:06 min, animator (dir. R. Kachanov)
	General Toptygin, puppets, 16:42 min, animator (dir. I. Ufimtsev)
1972	*Losharik* (*Little Horsey* – NB The character is a horse made up of little balls and the title is an untranslatable pun comprising these two elements), puppets, 10:18 min, animator (dir. I. Ufimtsev)
	Mama, puppets, 9:48 min, animator (dir. R. Kachanov)
	Novogodnaya skazka (*A New Year's Tale*), puppets, 17:36 min, animator (dir. V. Degtyarev)
1973	*Avrora* (*Aurora*), puppets, 18:24 min, animator (dir. R. Kachanov)
	Aibolit i Barmalei (*Aibolit and Barmalei*), puppets, 16:42 min, animator (dir. N. Chervinskaya)
	Lisa i zayats (*The Fox and the Hare*), cut-out, 12:24 min, director, animator
1974	*Pokhozhdeniya Chichikova: Manilov* (*The Adventures of Chichikov: Manilov*), puppets, 10:00 min, animator (dir. B. Stepantsev)

	Tsaplya i zhuravl (*The Heron and the Crane*), cut-out, 10:00 min, director, co-scriptwriter (with R. Kachanov), animator
	Shapoklyak (*Mrs Opera-Hat*), puppets, 19:48 min, animator (dir. R. Kachanov)
1975	*Yezhik v tumane* (*Hedgehog in the Fog*), cut-out, 10:29 min, director, animator
1976	*38 popugayev* (*38 Parrots*), puppets, 7:58 min, animator (dir. I. Ufimtsev)
1977	*Za den do nashei ery* (*One Day B.C.E.*), 4:00 min, montage of still photos with lighting effects (dir. F. Khitruk)
	Ya lechu k vam vospominaniyem (*I Fly to You in Memory* – Part 1 of Andrei Khrzhanovsky's *Pushkin Trilogy*), drawn and cut-out, 30:24 min, animator
1979	*Skazka skazok* (*Tale of Tales*), cut-out, 28:00 min, director, co-scriptwriter (with L. Petrushevskaya), animator
1980	*I s vami snova ya* (*I Am with You Again* – Part 2 of Khrzhanovsky's *Pushkin Trilogy*), drawn and cut-out, 30:06 min, animator
1981	*O sport, ty – mir* (*O Sport, You Are Peace*), live action feature (dir. Y. Ozerov) with animation section (dir. F. Khitruk), montage of still photos with lighting effects, prod. co. Mosfilm
	Production begun on *Shinel* (*The Overcoat*), now planned as 65:00 min, director, animator, co-scriptwriter (with L. Petrushevskaya), prod. co. Soyuzmultfilm, then Bykov Foundation, now Norstein Foundation
1982	*Osen* (*Autumn* – Part 3 of Khrzhanovsky's *Pushkin Trilogy*), drawn and cut-out, 42:00 min, animator
1994/95	*Russki Sakhar*, series of sugar commercials, cut-out and some drawn, 4 x 30 sec, director, scriptwriter, animator (design F. Yarbusova), prod. co. Norstein Foundation
2000	Opening titles for *Spokoinoi nochi, malyshi* (*Good Night Kids*), cut-out and some drawn, 2:00 min, director, scriptwriter (from an idea by M. Aldashin), animator (design V. Olshvang), for Channel 1 television, prod. co. Norstein Foundation
2003	A stanza of *Winter Days*, an international team project based on a collaborative poem led by Matsuo Basho, cut-out and some drawn, 1:37 min, director, scriptwriter, animator, for Imagica Entertainment Inc., Japan, prod. co. Norstein Foundation

All films are produced by Soyuzmultfilm, except where otherwise stated. Years are release dates except where otherwise stated.
This filmography is compiled from that published in *Animationsfilm sozialistischer Länder* (edited by Manfred Lichtenstein, with Klaus Lippert, Eckart Jahnke and Kurt Rohrmoser, Staatliches Filmarchiv der DDR, Berlin 1978), together with data from the animator.ru and soyuzmultfilm.ru websites and Norstein's recollections. English translations of titles are given for guidance only. I have consulted *Animationsfilm sozialistischer Länder* and synopses of films where available. I have not seen several of these films, and titles are notoriously hard to translate without intimate knowledge of the work.

Yuri Norstein Bibliography

Selected published texts written by Norstein and interviews with Norstein

'Simply Art', *Animafilm* 5 (1980), p. 40

'Pechal moya svetla ...', interview by V. Baranovsky in *Vechernyaya Odessa* 12.7.1980

'Multiplikatsiya rozhdayetsya tikho', interview by Zhanna Levitina, *Kino* (Lithuania) 6 (1982), p. 18

'Realnost, sozdannaya khudozhnikom', in *Mudrost vymisla*, ed. Sergei Asenin, Iskusstvo, Moscow 1983, p. 116

'Shinel. Po povesti N. V. Gogolya', *Overcoat* script plus interview by Tatyana Iensen in *Iskusstvo kino* 2 (1985), p. 81

'Za vidimoi kartinkoi na ekrane', interview by Mikhail Iampolski in *Problemy sinteza v khudozhestvennoi kulture*, Nauka, Moscow 1985, p. 149

'Sobor i kamni', interview by Mikhail Gurevich in *Sovetski ekran* 7 (1987), p. 16

'Priznaniye masteru', *Iskusstvo kino* 8 (1987), p. 74

'Snimal i "Shinel"...', interview by Maria Dementyeva in *Ogonek* 43 (1988), p. 17

'Dvizheniye ... Glavy iz nenapisannoi knigi', *Iskusstvo kino* 10 (1988), p. 103

'Dvizheniye ... 2. Poiski personazha', *Iskusstvo kino* 4 (1989), p. 107

'Tale of Tales: An Interview with Yuri Norstein in Budapest', interview by István Antal in supplement to *Le Quotidien*, Annecy International Animated Film Festival, 1989

'Iouri Norstein', interview by Michel Iampolski in *Cahiers du cinema* 47 (January 1990), Supplement on USSR, p. 39

Sotvoreniye filma, Natalya Venzher ed., Kinotsentr, Moscow 1990

'Prislushivayas k Norsteinu', *Az* 1 (1991), p. 18

'Vse eto bylo by smeshno', *Iskusstvo kino* 10 (1991), p. 139

'Yuri Norstein: Kavaler ordena iskusstv i literatury', interview by Tatyana Andriasova in *Moskovskiye novosti* no. 11, 14.3.1993

'Down the White Road', interview by Leslie Felperin Sharman in *Sight and Sound* 5 (1994), p. 20

'Metafory', *Iskusstvo kino* 7 (1994), p. 109

'Metafory' (continuation), *Iskusstvo kino* 8 (1994), p. 92

'Sneg na trave', *Iskusstvo kino* 9 (1999), p. 102

'Sneg na trave' (continuation), *Iskusstvo kino* 10 (1999), p. 98

'Norstein on Norstein and Russian Animation', interview by Stanislav Ulver in *Asifa News* vol. 13, 1 (2000), p. 6

'V pote litsa', *Iskusstvo kino* 12 (2000), p. 31

'Animacija je realistična kao san', interview by Midhat Ajan Ajanović in *Hrvatski filmski ljetopis* 29 (April 2002), p. 28

'Youri Norstein Biographie', interview by Totoro at Fougère Festival 16.5.2002, on DVDtoile.com web-site (http://dvdtoile.com/Filmographie.php?artiste+Youri+Norstein)

Franya i ya (catalogue for exhibition of work of Norstein and Yarbusova), Studio Ghibli, Tokyo 2003

'Kamera krupno-krupno priblizilas k cheloveku', interview by Alla Bossart in *Novaya Gazeta* 39, 2.6.2003 (http://2003.novayagazeta.ru/nomer/2003/39n/n39n-s37.shtml)

'Yuri Norstein. Na Tikusaya nishchego pokhozh', interview by Yelena Skulskaya in *Delo* 23.6.2003 (http://www.idelo.ru/282/26.html)

Selected published texts about or including references to Norstein

Arkadi Snesarev, 'We Introduce: Yuri Norstein', *Soviet Film* 6 (1976), p. 43

ed. Manfred Lichtenstein, with Klaus Lippert, Eckart Jahnke, Kurt Rohrmoser, *Animationsfilm sozialistischer Länder*, Staatliches Filmarchiv der DDR/Berlin 1978

M. Iampolski, 'Palitra i obyektiv', *Iskusstvo kino* 2 (1980), p. 94

Natalya Venzher, 'Zelenye yabloki na belom snegu', *Kino* (Latvia), December 1980, p. 9

T. Voronetskaya, 'Taina skazki', *Put k ekranu* 29 (1980)

N. Y. Venzher, *Soyuzmultfilm*, Soyuzinformkino, Moscow 1981, p. 31

Mikhail Yampolsky, 'The Space of the Animated Film: Khrzhanovsky's "I Am with You Again" and Norstein's "The Tale of Tales" ', trans. Andrew Braddel, *Afterimage* 13 (Autumn 1987), p. 104. Originally appeared in *Iskusstvo kino* 3 (1982), p. 92. NB The *Afterimage* article appeared before the author left Russia. He is now established in the United States and spells his name Iampolski rather than Yampolsky.

L. A. Karasev ed., *Rezhissery sovetskogo multiplikatsionnogo kino,* Soyuzinformkino, Moscow 1983, chapter on Norstein by Mikhail Iampolski, p. 19

Lyudmila Petrushevskaya, 'Rezhisser Yuri Norstein', *Sovetski film* 7 (1986), p. 9

Russell Taylor, 'Soviet Blocbusters', *1987 Bristol Animation Festival* catalogue

Karen Rosenberg, 'The Worldview of Youri Norstein: From a small flat in Moscow', *Animator* 28 (1988), p. 14

Raisa Fomina, 'Yuri Norstein: First Winner of the Andrey Tarkovsky Prize', *Soviet Film* 8 (1989), p. 2

Laurence Marks, 'A World Away from Bugs Bunny and Co', *Observer* 9.6.1991

Pavel Kryuchkov, 'Fioletovaya tetrad No. 39a: Vyd na Volgu – charlston razdayetsya', *Segodnya* 27 (1993)

Edwin Carels, 'Jurij Norstein in België', *Plateau* vol.11 no. 2, p. 4

A. M. Orlov, 'Kinostudiya "Soyuzmulfilm" segodnya', (http://www.aha.ru/~tkt/archive/10_99/multfilm.htm)

Jean Tiberi, Gustave de Staël, Alla Bossart, Yuri Norstein, Lyudmila Petrushevskaya, Emmanuel Daydé, Francesca Yarbusova, *Yuri Norstein, Francesca Yarbusova* (exhibition catalogue), Hôtel de Ville de Paris, Paris 2001

Useful web-sites

http://hedgehoginmist.narod.ru

http://www.soyuzmultfilm.ru

http://www.animator.ru

Films about Yuri Norstein

Youri Norstein: Un magicien de l'image, dir. Didier Deleskiewicz, prod. I.N.A., France 1984

Yuri Norstein, dir. Vichra Tarabanov, prod. Ecran TV Film Studio, Bulgaria 1991

Francesca Yarbusova, dir Vitali Troyanovsky, for Kultura TV channel, Russia 2003

Index

Norstein working on The Overcoat

Google Power

Unleash the Full Potential of Google

Chris Sherman

McGraw-Hill/Osborne

New York Chicago San Francisco Lisbon London Madrid Mexico City Milan New Delhi San Juan Seoul Singapore Sydney Toronto

The McGraw-Hill Companies

McGraw-Hill/Osborne
2100 Powell Street, 10th Floor
Emeryville, California 94608
U.S.A.

To arrange bulk purchase discounts for sales promotions, premiums, or fund-raisers, please contact **McGraw-Hill**/Osborne at the above address.

Google Power: Unleash the Full Potential of Google

1234567890 CUS CUS 0198765

ISBN 0-07-225787-3

Vice President & Group Publisher Philip Ruppel
Vice President & Publisher Jeffrey Krames
Acquisitions Editor Jane Brownlow
Project Editor Patty Mon
Acquisitions Coordinator Agatha Kim
Technical Editor Gary Price
Copy Editor Bart Reed
Proofreaders Paul Tyler, Stefany Otis
Indexer Valerie Robbins
Composition International Typesetting and Composition
Illustrator International Typesetting and Composition
Cover Design Pattie Lee

This book was composed with Adobe® InDesign®.